That's What SHE SAID!

366 Leadership Quotes
by Women

Compiled by

DR. JEANNE PORTER KING
WITH GABRIELLA LINDSAY

A Quote Book for Anyone Who Leads

© 2017 by Jeanne Porter King

Published by TransPorter Group Inc.
430 East 162nd Street, #441
South Holland, Illinois 60473

Printed in the United States of America

King, Jeanne Porter
That's What She Said: 366 Leadership Quotes by Women

ISBN-10: 0-692-85024-4
ISBN-13: 978-0-692-85024-4

To my nieces

Kristen, Kiara, Kiandria, and Taylor

Be inspired to lead.
Use your voice to speak courageously
and confidently about the things that matter in our world.

CONTENTS

INTRODUCTION

WOMEN'S WORDS MATTER.

But they can be too easily discounted in every culture across the globe, especially in popular culture. Take the popular Internet meme "That's what she said." The phrase is a double entendre that has sexual undertones. Its American origin goes back as far as 1929 in a test reel for an Alfred Hitchcock movie; made popular by the 1992 comedy *Wayne's World* and the television sitcom *The Office*, it was formally defined in 2003.[1]

At least four "That's What She Said (TWSS)" apps are listed in Apple's app store. Here's the description from one such app: "Turn any discussion into a funny and often obscene joke!"[2] Women's words are too important to be relegated to the sophomoric stereotypes of crude and rude.

Women's words are no laughing matter. Women have important things to say about crucial topics. Yet we know that popular culture informs and shapes attitudes about so much of life, including women's lives. Popular culture perpetuates stereotypes about women, and these stereotypes creep into our places of work and worship, as well as our homes and communities. It is important that women re-appropriate and redirect these memes, so that what "she" says is not used to signify sexual or obscene content but instead advances the causes of women, our communities, our families, and our world.

When "she" speaks, we want her words to be taken seriously, for the sake of our daughters and our sons, and our colleagues and

---

1 http://knowyourmeme.com/memes/thats-what-she-said, https://www.thrillist.com/news/nation/origin-history-of-thats-what-she-said

2 That's What She Said by Mike Matz https://appstore.re/us/1lais.i

5

our managers—both male and female. We want our businesses and community institutions to value the words of women.

This book is composed of the courageous, sometimes countercultural words of women on the topic of leadership and leading. Let's face it, for eons, men have been considered the sages on leadership. Though women leadership scholars and practitioners have increased in the past two decades, the implicit associations of leadership are still predominantly male.

In 2005, Catalyst Inc., a research-based women's advocacy and consultancy group, published a report[3] showing how business leaders held to stereotypes that women are better at leading according to a relational, nurturing style. Catalyst termed this relational style as "Take Care" leadership. Men, however, were seen by the business leaders who were surveyed to excel at "Take Charge" leadership. In most organizations, "Take Charge" leadership is seen as strategic and results-oriented, and it is implicit to the notions of leadership that get rewarded for advancement. There is no empirical evidence to support the idea that women cannot take charge or that men can't take care. That stereotypic view of leadership plays a huge role in limiting women's leadership advancement.

These implicit gendered associations are still operative today. In their book *Blindspot: Hidden Biases of Good People*, Mahzarin Banaji and Anthony Greenwald review studies and experiments that document how unconscious mental functions impact human behavior. In fact, Dr. Greenwald developed an automated sorting task to measure implicit or unconscious associations we hold. This sorting task is now known as the Implicit Associations Test (IAT). Two IATs of the many tests they've developed are particularly relevant to how women and men are viewed: the Gender-Science IAT and the Gender-Career IAT. According to Harvard's Implicit site, where anyone can take one of the IATS, the Gender-Science IAT "often reveals a relative link between liberal arts and females and between science and males;" and

---

3 http://www.catalyst.org/knowledge/women-take-care-men-take-charge-stereotyping-us-business-leaders-exposed

6

the Gender-Career IAT "often reveals a relative link between family and females and between career and males."[4]

The American Association of University Women (AAUW) is the nation's leading voice promoting equity and education for women and girls. AAUW has collaborated with Project Implicit and Harvard University researchers to create a test that looks at the mental associations we make between gender and a variety of concepts, many of which affect our beliefs about women in positions of leadership. AAUW's report, *Barriers and Bias: The Status of Women In Leadership*, reviews the literature around gender stereotypes and leadership. The research they reviewed shows that the "stereotypes associated with leadership are decidedly masculine" and "correlate with current expectations of leadership." These expectations, the authors of the report go on to say, "affect women's and men's self-perceptions."[5] In other words, stereotypes have consequences and create a perpetuating cycle.

This book, *That's What She Said! 366 Leadership Quotes by Women*, adds women's voices to the leadership narrative and aims, with our words, to dispel stereotypes about women and leadership. Women are taking charge of our representations, the memes and themes about us, and using our own words to share our wisdom. This book intentionally appropriates an Internet meme that many of us see as demeaning to women and reinvigorates it for the purposes of celebrating, affirming, and advancing women's leadership.

This book uses the meme much the same way that Oprah Winfrey used it when speaking with then First Lady Michelle Obama in Obama's last televised interview from the White House. Both were seated comfortably in front of the camera as if two girlfriends conversing about their lives. Oprah started with a series of questions about how Mrs. Obama handled the challenges she faced in the two terms her husband served as president of the United States. In many ways, race

---

4 https://implicit.harvard.edu/implicit/selectatest.html
5 AAUW, Barriers and Bias, pp. 22-23.

7

was a subtext to those challenges; they both knew it. However, Mrs. Obama was too gracious to name it explicitly. So Oprah read a lengthy excerpt of a *New York Times* piece written in tribute to Mrs. Obama by award-winning Nigerian novelist and feminist apologist Chimamanda Ngozi Adichie:

> Because she said what she thought and because she smiled only when she felt like smiling, and not constantly and vacuously, America's cheapest caricature was cast on her, the angry black woman.[6]

Mrs. Obama let out a sound, part *hmm* and part *ha ha*. It was not laughter but the sound that emits from a woman's soul when her womanhood has been defended. In Mrs. Obama's case, the sound was in response to the truth about the assault on her as a black woman.

To Mrs. Obama's nonverbal acknowledgment of a truth, Oprah, with just enough sassiness in her tone, and her face fixed as if to dare anyone to challenge that statement, replied, "*mmm hmmm, that's what she said!*" To which Mrs. Obama confidently replied, "She said it well, too!"

That exchange between the former First Lady and America's interview queen, signified an agreement with a heretofore unstated knowing that Ms. Adichie put in words. It signified what many of us well knew: Without personally meeting Mrs. Obama, too many people across the U.S. had placed her in a stereotypical box. Had she called it out while in office, she would have been labeled a complainer, a whiner playing the race card. So Ms. Adichie spoke truth, to which we echo Oprah's words with our own strong conviction, "That's what she said!"

It is in that spirit that this book of quotes is offered. When the formal narrative about leadership is still male dominated, women across the world have important things to say about leadership that

---

6 https://www.nytimes.com/2016/10/17/t-magazine/michelle-obama-chimamanda-ngozi-adichie-gloria-steinem-letter.html?_r=0

speak of a general understanding of leadership as well as women's distinct perspective on leading.

We've gathered this collection of quotes from women that represent a diverse array of experiences: from women who are CEOs of Fortune 500 companies to women who are ecclesiastical leaders in various faith traditions. We've included academics, entertainers, athletes, educators, writers; women from various countries, ethnic, racial, and cultural backgrounds; young women and more experienced women; famous and not-so-famous women; and infamous women. All have something to say about women's leadership!

That's What She Said! is a celebration and affirmation of women's words on leadership. We dare speak our own truth about power, confidence, communication, purposefulness, collaboration, and support because our words do matter.

We provide you with 366 quotes—one for every day, including Leap Year. I encourage you to read each quote, jot down your reflections on the topics; and by all means, share what women have said on these topics. We've also included a short bio on each woman we've quoted, because not only do our words matter, but we also matter as women. We matter, not merely as sexual beings but as agents of our own and others' destinies. We matter as leaders. We matter as curators of ideas. Our voices matter to shaping the leadership of this and ensuing generations.

May this book inspire you to use your voice to speak courageously and confidently about the things that matter in our world.

DEFINING LEADERSHIP

Leadership is a cultural phenomenon.

It is a process in which leaders provide direction, guidance, organization, connection, sense-making, and even meaning to members of corporations, community organizations, churches, political movements, and government bureaucracies. Leaders exist at all levels of these organizations and institutions. Historically, women were omitted from or under-represented in the formal leadership narrative—that is the books, journal articles, the places where leadership practices and principles were shared. But that has changed. Women lead at all levels of every type of organization—from Fortune 500 companies to senate and congressional committees to political movements. And women write, speak, and teach about leadership in profound ways! Women's perspectives and experiences of leadership are invaluable to all of us who lead wherever we lead.

1

1

Leaders do not ask for the task, but are tracked down by the spirit of the times until it consumes them; they reach a point where they become the symbol of the disaffected and the movement swirling around them.
~Coretta Scott King~

2

A leader is one who sees the whole situation, organizes the experiences of the group, offers a vision of the future, and trains followers to be leaders.
~Rosabeth Moss Kanter~

3

A leader takes people where they want to go. A great leader takes people where they don't necessarily want to go but ought to be.
~Rosalynn Carter~

4

If your actions create a legacy that inspires others to dream more, learn more, do more and become more, then, you are an excellent leader.
~Dolly Parton~

5
A good leader is someone who sees beyond themselves and really thinks about how they can move their organization forward by helping others to fulfill their potential.
~Sharon Allen~

6
To have a great leader you must have eager followers.
~Pat Summit's team saying~

7
The great thing about leadership is that it can be done in so many different ways. It doesn't have to be predefined; it doesn't have to be packaged. It's important for people, and especially women, to recognize that.
~Sharon Allen~

8
Women are leaders everywhere you look—from the CEO who runs a Fortune 500 company to the housewife who raises her children and heads her household. Our country was built by strong women, and we will continue to break down walls and defy stereotypes.
~Nancy Pelosi~

9

I am endlessly fascinated that playing football is
considered a training ground for leadership,
but raising children isn't.
~Dee Dee Myers~

10

Good leaders inspire others to have confidence in their
leader. Great leaders inspire others to have confidence
in themselves.
~Eleanor Roosevelt~

11

The images and pictures that come to mind when we
think "leader" speak volumes about our unspoken—
yet prevailing—ideals of leadership. If we want to
expand our concept of leadership, we need to expand
our images of who and what a leader is.
~Dr. Jeanne Porter King~

12

Leadership is really a form of temporary authority that
others grant you, and they only follow you if they find
you consistently credible.
~Pat Summit~

13

I know of no single formula for success. But over
the years I have observed that some attributes of
leadership are universal and are often about finding
ways of encouraging people to combine their efforts,
their talents, their insights, their enthusiasm and their
inspiration to work together.
~Queen Elizabeth II~

14

Leadership should be more participative than directive,
more enabling than performing.
~Mary D. Poole~

15

As a leader, it's a major responsibility on your shoulders to
practice the behavior you want others to follow.
~Himanshu Bhatia~

16

You have to look at leadership through the eyes of the
followers and you have to live the message. What I have
learned is that people become motivated when you guide
them to the source of their own power and when you
make heroes out of employees who personify what you
want to see in the organization.
~Anita Roddick~

17

Women like me tend to always look over their
shoulder to see who… "Who's the leader? Who's the
smart one?" Never thinking it might be ME. Took a
long time for me to get over that.
~Jane Fonda~

18

The most important role of a leader is to set a clear
direction, be transparent about how to get there, and to
stay the course.
~Irene Rosenfeld~

19

Leadership is about making others better as a result of
your presence, making sure that impact lasts in your
absence.
~Sheryl Sandberg~

20

Most people don't realize that leadership is
fundamentally about service, about dying to self and
loving others into their true potential.
~Binta Niambi Brown~

21
Leaders work on existing paradigms; managers work within existing paradigms.
~*Bishop Vashti McKenzie*~

22
Good leaders are always trying to enrich their tool kits. Great leaders know what tools to use when.
~*Marsha Clark*~

23
For a leader, the promised land is something that you see and know and that can't be beaten out of you even when other people don't see it yet—even when they say it is impossible, unrealistic, idealistic.
~*Ruth Haley Barton*~

24
Leadership is asking a lot of questions. I've learned that between customers, employees and all our stakeholders, my number one job is asking [my team] a lot of questions so I can serve them.
~*Monif Clarke*~

25

Now as our understanding of leadership has evolved, we can examine their stories through a different lens. The distinct leadership styles of these courageous and skillful women point us toward new images of leadership: ways of talking about and seeing leadership that honor women's experiences and perspectives.
~Dr. Jeanne Porter King~

26

[A leader is] someone who unites people to work towards a common goal. A leader is someone who creates collaboration.
~Ellen Johnson Sirleaf~

27

Lee Iacocca famously asked, "Where have all the leaders gone?" The answer of course, is that we're all leaders. Every one of us has the power to inspire people around us to change what has always been.
~C. Vivian Stringer~

28

[Leadership] is all about perception—and if teammates find you the least bit inconsistent, moody, unpredictable, indecisive, or emotionally unreliable, then they balk and the whole team is destabilized.
~Pat Summit~

29

Being a leader is actually being completely with who you are and speaking from that place, giving feedback, sharing opinions from that place. That's why people follow you.
~Danae Ringelmann~

30

A willingness to do whatever it is that needs to be done regardless of self-interest is the hallmark of a mature leader.
~Pat Summit~

31

The hard knocks prepare one for leadership as much as the soft landings.
~Coretta Scott King~

32

There is no room [in the world] for mediocre women. You have to work. You have to work exceptionally hard, and you have to know what you're talking about.
~Madeline Albright~

33
Good leaders are mindful of what makes employees
feel included—and excluded.
~Deborah Gillis~

34
The best leaders know that employees would rather
work for people who recognize and value the talents of
others—and are honest about their own shortcomings.
~Deborah Gillis~

35
Real leaders don't issue edicts just to look and sound
like they're in charge. Real leaders listen, gather critical
information, weigh the options carefully, look for a
timely opening (typically when everyone else is writhing
in indecision), and then demand action.
~Sylvia Ann Hewlett~

36
We're not naturally born knowing how to be leaders.
Instead, leadership is a skill that is built as the result of
thousands and thousands of micro-lessons over the
course of a career.
~Sallie Krawcheck~

37

At the heart of leadership is having the ability to articulate a vision such that others buy into it, work consistently towards it, and at the end of the day, produce results.
~Dr. Avis A. Jones-Deweever~

38

Problem is, what looks and sounds like leadership coming from a man, can be interpreted completely differently, coming from a woman.
~Dr. Avis A. Jones-Deweever~

39

A good leader is someone who can remain strong even in difficult and trying circumstances; someone who is empowering those around them; and someone who is as interested in the needs of the people they work with and the larger needs of the project or the organization as they are in their own needs.
~Leslie Lewin~

40

Leadership is being a standard-bearer for causes that don't matter to the establishment.
~Dr. Denise Dresser~

41

Good leaders organize and align people around what the team needs to do. Great leaders motivate and inspire people with why they're doing it. That's purpose. And that's the key to achieving something truly transformational.

~Marillyn Hewson~

42

Leadership is hard to define and good leadership even harder. But if you can get people to follow you to the ends of the earth, you are a great leader.

~Indra Nooyi~

43

Leadership is a series of behaviors rather than a role for heroes.

~Margaret Wheatley~

44

Leadership is about presenting confidence and decisiveness.

~Anne Fulenwider~

45

Leadership is something that is learned. It can be learned and should be learned. Leadership is something you're always honing and learning and reflecting to see ways you could have been better at it. Anyone who thinks they're a natural leader is probably horrible to work with.
~Rachel Sklar~

46

I want every little girl who's told she is bossy to be told she has leadership skills.
~Sheryl Sandburg~

47

If you are generous with the "attaboys" or "attagirls" for the people on your team, particularly if you are in a position of authority, and you are known for using words such as we and us rather than I or me, then you'll be seen as a great leader for whom people would want to work.
~Carla A. Harris~

48

Leadership is a responsibility shared by all members of the organization.
~Frances Hesselbein~

49

Lead from the front; don't push from the rear.
~*Frances Hesselbein*~

INFLUENTIAL
LEADERSHIP

Leaders are influencers.

Influence is power in action. It is the ability to get things done, however, without overpowering others. It is power in service of others, the organizations, or institutions in which we work and serve. It is power in service to the greater good. Influence is primarily an interpersonal process that extends to our ability to make impact on groups, organizations, and our broader social networks. Influential leaders make impact on others.

2

50

Influence often seems so wishy-washy when compared with the assumptions that power is absolute. Influence is what women can have when they do not have power. If we want to change the world, we need both ... influence can be powerful and change culture.
~Wendy McCarthy~

51

I believe influence is the union of power and purpose.
~Dr. Condoleezza Rice~

52

Influence can be defined as earning the right to be heard so that others are moved toward their best. Like salt shaken out influence is hard to see, but its flavor is impossible to miss.
~Pam Farrel~

53

The key is that women (and men) in position to influence others — either by virtue of the title they hold in an organization or because they have gained the necessary skills, insight and confidence — create the conditions under which many more people can and will lead within their broadly defined spheres of influence.
~Nancy Dearman~

54
Trust is the conduit for influence; it's the medium through which ideas travel.
~Amy Cuddy~

55
Give light and people will find the way.
~Ella Baker~

56
If you think you're too small to have an impact, try going to bed with a mosquito.
~Anita Roddick~

57
Never underestimate the power of dreams and the influence of the human spirit. We are all the same in this notion: The potential for greatness lives within each of us.
~Wilma Rudolph~

58

You may not always have a comfortable life and you will not always be able to solve all of the world's problems at once but don't ever underestimate the importance you can have because history has shown us that courage can be contagious and hope can take on a life of its own.
~*Michelle Obama*~

59

I hold that a strongly marked personality can influence descendants for generations.
~*Beatrix Potter*~

60

You are here to make a difference, to either improve the world or worsen it. And whether or not you consciously choose to, you will accomplish one or the other.
~*Richelle E. Goodrich*~

61

Never underestimate the influence you have on others.
~*Dr. Laurie Buchanan*~

62
When the whole world is silent, even one voice
becomes powerful.
~*Malala Yousafzai*~

63
Our life ripples out, and it has influence. That's why
it's important that we're at our best and that we're
influencing others for the good.
~*Victoria Osteen*~

64
Power is a tool, influence is a skill; one is a fist, the
other a fingertip.
~*Nancy Gibbs*~

65
Wherever you are, that's your stage, your circle
of influence. That's your talk show, that's where
your power lies.... You have the power to change
somebody's life. Everyone has a calling, and your real
job in life is to figure out what that is and get about the
business of doing it.
~*Oprah Winfrey*~

66
I wouldn't ask anyone to do anything I wouldn't do myself.
~Indra Nooyi~

67
Blessed is the influence of one true, loving human soul on another.
~George Eliot (Mary Ann Evans)~

68
You can't live in a global society, let alone lead in it, if you don't know anything about it.
~Dr. Charleyse Pratt~

69
We treat our people like royalty. If you honor and serve the people who work for you, they will honor and serve you.
~Mary Kay Ash~

70
How wonderful it is that nobody need wait a single moment before starting to improve the world.
~Anne Frank~

71

The goal is to find work where one can do the greatest social good with the least amount of psychic damage to one's self. #vocation
~Dr. Renita Weems~

72

We are all here for a reason. I believe the reason is to throw little torches out to lead people through the dark.
~Whoopi Goldberg~

73

I've learned that people will forget what you said, people will forget what you did, but people will never forget how you made them feel.
~Maya Angelou~

74

There are two ways of spreading light: to be the candle or the mirror that reflects it.
~Edith Wharton~

75

As you grow older, you will realize you have two hands, one for helping yourself, one for helping others.
~Audrey Hepburn~

76

To handle yourself, use your head; to handle others, use your heart.
~*Eleanor Roosevelt*~

77

Success isn't about how much money you make. It's about the difference you make in people's lives.
~*Michelle Obama*~

78

Let us remember: One book, one pen, one child, and one teacher can change the world.
~*Malala Yousafzai*~

79

Memories of our lives, of our works, and our deeds will continue in others.
~*Rosa Parks*~

80

We are here ... to influence the world, rather than to be influenced by the world.
~*Sheri L. Dew*~

81

I always believed that one woman's success can only help another woman's success.
~*Gloria Vanderbilt*~

82

If you were born with the ability to change someone's perspective or emotions, never waste that gift. It is one of the most powerful gifts God can give—the ability to influence.
~*Shannon L. Alder*~

83

It's good to toss in a stone and begin your own ripple of influence.
~*Joy Cooper*~

84

You really can change the world if you care enough.
~*Marian Wright Edelman*~

85

I am excited to use [blogging] as a tool to not only share my story, but to empower other women who are faced with that deep burning for more, who see things in their dreams and yearn to make them a reality. Women who, like me, contemplate taking that leap but are fearful of the ground below. Trust me, the net is there, it will catch you, and you will survive the jump. I won't lie, likely you will not come out unscathed, but don't those bumps and bruises only make us that much stronger?
~Gabriella Lindsay~

86

You teach a little by what you say. You teach most by what you are.
~Henrietta Mears~

87

We ought always to try to influence others for good.
~Lucy Maud Montgomery~

88

If you have knowledge, let others light their candles in it.
~Margaret Fuller~

89
Any one of us can be a rainbow in somebody's clouds.
~ Maya Angelou~

90
As we let our own light shine, we unconsciously give other people permission to do the same.
~ Marianne Williamson~

91
For what is done or learned by one class of women becomes, by virtue of their common womanhood, the property of all women.
~Elizabeth Blackwell~

92
Our hesitancy to take credit for our accomplishments results in a loss of power, influence, and political capital in the workplace.
~Bonnie Marcus~

93
No matter how senior you get in an organization, no matter how well you're perceived to be doing, your job is never done.
~Abigail Johnson~

94
People respond well to those that are sure of what they want.
~Anna Wintour~

95
There will be some people in your sphere of influence who have been waiting for you to step out, so they can step out and be real, too.
~Dr. Cynthia Hale~

AUTHENTIC LEADERSHIP

Leadership is personal; it starts with the self.

Leadership starts on the inside and works its way out to a distinct type of interaction with others. Leadership is as much about character as it is competence and convictions. How we lead is connected to who we are deep within. Leaders grapple with the tensions of authenticity and authority, of being liked and being respected, of being assertive but not aggressive, of being confident but not overconfident. The leader must have a strong sense of herself—what she has done and can do. She must be self-aware, and clear on who she is and what she is called to do.

3

96

Don't be afraid to be you and own it.
~Danae Ringelmann~

97

No one can make you feel inferior without your consent.
~Eleanor Roosevelt~

98

The primary responsibility for defining one's own
reality lies with the people who live that reality, who
actually have those experiences.
~Patricia Hill Collins~

99

I began to understand that each crisis, even each new
heartache, was just preparation for the leadership role
that I would have in the coming years.
~Coretta Scott King~

100

You know, if you just set out to be liked, you would be
prepared to compromise on anything, wouldn't you, at
any time? And you would achieve nothing!
~Margaret Thatcher~

101
Lead on with light.
~Gloria Naylor~

102
If you do not have confidence in yourself, how can you expect others to have confidence in you?
~Nora Wu~

103
Confidence is a sweet spot between arrogance and despair. Arrogance involves the failure to see any flaws or weaknesses, despair the failure to acknowledge any strengths.
~Rosabeth Moss Kanter~

104
The decisions others make may impact your life, sometimes even in negative, heart-breaking ways. But their decisions don't have the power to alter the essence of who you are.
~Dr. Renita Weems~

105
You lead with much more true confidence when you understand how people around you—whether they agree or disagree with your decision—will react. In that way, you'll be able to pull them along with you even if they don't agree with you.
~Katie Rae~

106
When you're comfortable and content with who you are, the voices of others who try and define, control, or direct you are not important.
~Rachel Robins~

107
Until you believe you can do it, it's going to be difficult to convince anyone else you can do it.
~Toni Sorenson~

108
Confidence consists of positive expectations for favorable outcomes.
~Rosabeth Moss Kanter~

109

A woman with a voice is by definition a strong woman.
~*Melinda Gates*~

110

Women are not more moral than men ... we don't have
our masculinity to prove.
~*Gloria Steinem*~

111

I will urge you to transform, to find your voice and
then work on your legacy. We can be so busy looking
back that we miss what's before us.
~*Dr. Charleyse Pratt*~

112

Presenting leadership as a list of carefully defined
qualities (like strategic, analytical and performance-
oriented) no longer holds. Instead, true leadership
stems from individuality that is honestly and sometimes
imperfectly expressed.... Leaders should strive for
authenticity over perfection.
~*Sheryl Sandberg*~

113

I have a lot of stamina, and I have a lot of resilience.
~Hillary Clinton~

114

If people trust you as a person, they will trust you as
a leader ... and that's an important component that
some leaders don't ever get to.
~Sharon Allen~

115

Sometimes women try to define their own leadership
style by looking too much at those around them—and
many times those people are men. Finding your own
way to provide leadership is one of the most important
discoveries that we find as we evolve in our careers.
~Sharon Allen~

116

A woman is like a tea bag—you never know how
strong it is until it's in hot water.
~Eleanor Roosevelt~

117
It took me quite a long time to develop a voice,
and now that I have it, I am not going to be silent.
~Madeleine Albright~

118
As I grew older, I started to realize we were all born
to stand out; nobody is born to blend in. How boring
would this be if everyone was the same.
~Halima Aden~

119
I've never met a woman who is not strong, but
sometimes they don't let it out. Then there's a tragedy,
and then all of a sudden that strength comes. My
message is let the strength come out before the tragedy.
~Diane von Furstenberg~

120
Take criticism seriously but not personally. If there
is truth or merit in the criticism, try to learn from it.
Otherwise, let it roll right off you.
~Hillary Clinton~

121

Women will only have true equality when men share with them the responsibility of bringing up the next generation.
~Ruth Bader Ginsburg~

122

We need to start work with the idea that we're going to learn every day. I learn, even at my position, every single day.
~Chanda Kochhar~

123

No person is your friend (or kin) who demands your silence, or denies your right to grow and be perceived as fully blossomed as you were intended. Or who belittles in any fashion the gifts you labor so to bring into the world.
~Alice Walker~

124

Don't limit yourself. Many people limit themselves to what they think they can do. You can go as far as your mind lets you. What you believe, remember, you can achieve.
~Mary Kay Ash~

125

Each of us has the right and the responsibility to assess the roads which lie ahead and…if the future road looms ominous or unpromising … then we need to gather our resolve and … step off … into another direction.
~Maya Angelou~

126

I wasn't out giving speeches and marching and all of that. In my view you have to have women do that, but you also have to have women accomplish the goal and be the role model. So I tried to be the role model and be the rabbi.
~Rabbi Sally Priesand~

127

Understanding who you are is critical for your career advancement. Self-awareness helps you get ahead.
~Bonnie Marcus~

128

Doubt is a killer. You just have to know who you are and what you stand for.
~Jennifer Lopez~

129

Don't waste your energy trying to change opinions ...
do your thing, and don't care if they like it.
~Tina Fey~

130

Power's not given to you. You have to take it.
~Beyoncé Knowles-Carter~

131

Low self-confidence isn't a life sentence. Self-
confidence can be learned, practiced, and mastered—
just like any other skill. Once you master it, everything
in your life will change for the better.
~Barrie Davenport~

132

The most beautiful thing you can wear is confidence.
~Blake Lively~

133

Life is not easy for any of us. But what of that? We
must have perseverance and above all confidence
in ourselves. We must believe that we are gifted for
something and that this thing must be attained.
~Marie Curie~

134

Love who you are, embrace who you are. Love yourself. When you love yourself, people can kind of pick up on that: they can see confidence, they can see self-esteem, and naturally, people gravitate towards you.
~*Lilly Singh*~

135

Whatever we believe about ourselves and our ability comes true for us.
~*Susan L. Taylor*~

136

People are like stained-glass windows. They sparkle and shine when the sun is out, but when the darkness sets in their true beauty is revealed only if there is light from within.
~*Elisabeth Kubler-Ross*~

137

We cannot do everything, and there is a sense of liberation in realizing that. This enables us to do something, and to do it very well.
~*Ruth Haley Barton*~

138

Character cannot be developed in ease and quiet. Only through experiences of trial and suffering can the soul be strengthened, vision cleared, ambition inspired, and success achieved.
~Helen Keller~

139

It turns out that becoming a leader and doing something amazing with your life hinge on what makes you different, not on what makes you the same as everyone else.
~Sylvia Ann Hewlett~

140

It's about signaling that you have not only depth and heft but also the confidence and credibility to get your point across and create buy-in when the going gets rough—when your enterprise or venture is under extreme pressure.
~Sylvia Ann Hewlett~

141

The leader for today and the future will be focused on how to be—how to develop quality, character, mind-set, values, principles, and courage.

~Frances Hesselbein~

142
But in the professional context, fear kills dreams. It will keep you stuck in the sanctuary of the familiar and secluded from your greatest potential. To reach your biggest and boldest leadership ambitions, you either learn to master fear or fear will become your master.
~Dr. Avis A. Jones-Deweever~

143
My grandmother would always say to us, "Cover all the ground you stand on," that meant having clarity about who you are, where you come from and conducting yourself in a way that allows you to show your self-confidence and not arrogance.
~Connie Lindsey~

144
In order to stay focused on remaining authentic and being the best original you can be, you must first understand what your competitive strengths are and concentrate on improving your weaknesses.
~Carla A. Harris~

COURAGEOUS LEADERSHIP

Leaders must face their fear and move forward anyway.

In so many ways leadership is an act of faith—moving people into an unknown future. Leaders must garner the courage to move people forward in spite of obstacles, resistance, and dissent. The courageous leader has to be bold when she doesn't necessarily feel bold. The courageous leader will have to take stands that run counter to popular opinion and must find the strength to do what is right, to speak truth when others are silent.

4

145

You can waste your lives drawing lines. Or you can live
your life crossing them.
~*Shonda Rhimes*~

146

Sometimes you just have to make a leap of faith. As
I was moving up the ranks, sometimes I'd be in a
meeting and think, "We really need to make a decision
here," and realize a beat later it was me who had to
make that decision.
~*Anne Fulenwider*~

147

Indeed, this life is a test. It is a test of many things—
of our convictions and priorities, our faith and our
faithfulness, our patience and our resilience, and in the
end, our ultimate desires.
~*Sheri L. Dew*~

148

Each of us has the right, that possibility, to invent
ourselves daily. If a person does not invent herself, she
will be invented. So, to be bodacious enough to invent
ourselves is wise.
~*Maya Angelou*~

149

Noble and great. Courageous and determined. Faithful and fearless. That is who you are and who you have always been. And understanding it can change your life, because this knowledge carries a confidence that cannot be duplicated any other way.
~*Sheri L. Dew*~

150

So I would wish for my younger sisters courage. That would include speaking up and speaking out whenever they encounter injustice, whenever their humanness is being challenged, ridiculed, or questioned....
Passion to me is timeless.
~*Dr. Johnnetta B. Cole*~

151

You must commit to yourself to be unwavering in your determination not to give others the power to define your future, limit your vision, or in any way, set parameters on what you know to be the full breadth of your personal possibilities.
~*Dr. Avis A. Jones-Deweever*~

152
You gain strength, courage, and confidence by every experience in which you really stop to look fear in the face. You are able to say to yourself, "I lived through this horror. I can take the next thing that comes along."
~*Eleanor Roosevelt*~

153
Have the courage of your convictions—no matter what the challenges are. And by all means, choose your battlefields.
~*Her Excellency, Ellen Johnson Sirleaf*~

154
I was once afraid of people saying, "Who does she think she is?" Now I have the courage to stand and say, "This is who I am."
~*Oprah Winfrey*~

155
Just remember, you can do anything you set your mind to, but it takes action, perseverance, and facing your fears.
~*Gillian Anderson*~

156

When we speak we are afraid our words will not be heard or welcomed. But when we are silent, we are still afraid. So it is better to speak.
~Audre Lorde~

157

I have stood on a mountain of no's for one yes.
~B. Smith~

158

If you really feel strongly about something, have the courage to defend what you're suggesting.
~Indra Nooyi~

159

Responsibility to yourself means refusing to let others do your thinking, talking, and naming for you; it means learning to respect and use your own brains and instincts; hence, grappling with hard work.
~Adrienne Rich~

160

People say I'm so controversial. But I think the most controversial thing I've done is to stick around.
~Madonna~

161

I have learned over the years that when one's mind is made up, this diminishes fear; knowing what must be done does away with fear.

~Rosa Parks~

162

Be courageous, ask for what you want and be specific. Think boldly, dream your biggest dreams and believe you are worthy of achieving them.

You are enough!

~Connie Lindsey~

POWER-FULL LEADERSHIP

Power is the ability to influence.

It is the ability to make an impact on others. It is the ability to shape the direction of organizations and nations. Power is what enables us to get things done and to make things happen. Existing and emerging leaders need power and need to know how to use it wisely in their organizations. The good news is, whether you realize it or not you have power and can use it. You need to learn how to leverage it and expand it for the good of all. The leader must own her power and then use it to advance in structural power and expand her social power. Her aim must be to use "power-with" instead of "power-over" strategies to grow her leadership and to help others own and use their power for the good of all.

5

163

Power might be defined as simply the ability to make things happen, to be a causal agent, to initiate change.
~Mary Parker Follett~

164

It seems to me that whereas power usually means power-over, the power of some person or group over some other person or group, it is possible to develop a conception of power-with, a jointly developed power, a co-active, not a coercive power.
~Mary Parker Follett~

165

We do not need magic to change the world; we carry all the power we need inside ourselves already: we have the power to imagine better.
~J.K. Rowling~

166

When someone is cruel or acts like a bully, you don't stoop to their level. No, our motto is
"When they go low, we go high."
~Michelle Obama~

167

I think every individual has his or her own power, and it's a matter of working, taking time and defining what that power is.
~Jill Scott~

168

Unless you choose to do great things with it, it makes no difference how much you are rewarded, or how much power you have.
~Oprah Winfrey~

169

Truly powerful people have great humility. They do not try to impress, they do not try to be influential. They simply are.... They never persuade, nor do they use manipulation or aggressiveness to get their way. They listen. If there is anything they can offer to assist you, they offer it.
~Sanaya Roman~

170

Sometimes the words people don't say are as powerful as the ones they do.
~Ann E. Burg~

171

Sometimes, reaching out and taking someone's hand is the beginning of a journey. At other times, it is allowing another to take yours.
~*Vera Nazarian*~

172

Leaders in all realms and activities of life knew that the power they had come to hold existed because they were responsible to serve the many, thus power was position of service.
~*Vanna Bonta*~

173

A choir is made up of many voices, including yours and mine. If one by one all go silent, then all that will be left are the soloists. Don't let a loud few determine the nature of the sound. It makes for poor harmony and diminishes the song.
~*Vera Nazarian*~

174

We can only reach the highest height if we encourage each other.
~*Lailah Gifty Akita*~

175

Women lead in different ways. Women rarely feel the
need to speak the most at a meeting to make a point.
~Patricia Bellinger~

176

We as women … underestimate ourselves. I'm pretty
smart. I work pretty hard. I'm good at what I do. I
have really good instincts. I have great ideas. And I
can execute. I say that out loud because we as women
don't pat ourselves on the back. We're always sort of
deferring. We cede our power so easily.
~Michelle Obama~

177

Women don't realize how powerful they are.
~Judith Light~

178

It's not about supplication; it's about power. It's not
about asking; it's about demanding. It's not about
convincing those who are currently in power; it's about
changing the very face of power itself.
~Kimberle Williams Crenshaw~

179
Do the best you can in every task, no matter how unimportant it may seem at the time. No one learns more about a problem than the person at the bottom.
~Sandra Day O'Connor~

180
It is important for you not only to see who you can become, but to know that you are empowered to become what you see.
~Dr. Cynthia Hale~

181
Progress comes from caring more about what needs to be done than about who gets the credit.
~Dr. Dorothy Height~

182
There's a time that may come in an organization where leading by influence is not enough. When things are not going the way they need to go, there's a time when one has to step up ... to set the organization back on the right direction.
~Abigail Johnson~

183

Power is nothing unless you can turn it into influence.
~Condoleezza Rice~

184

Power to me is the ability to make a change in a
positive way.
~Victoria Justice~

185

The most common way people give up their power is
thinking they don't have any.
~Alice Walker~

186

Women have to harness their power—it's absolutely
true. It's just learning not to take the first no. And if
you can't go straight ahead, you go around the corner.
~Cher~

187

When I dare to be powerful, to use my strength in the
service of my vision, then it becomes less and less
important whether I am afraid.
~Audre Lorde~

188
We still think of a powerful man as a born leader and a powerful woman as an anomaly.
~Margaret Atwood~

189
Do not wait on a leader ... look in the mirror, it's you!
~Katherine Miracle~

190
A wise woman wishes to be no one's enemy; a wise woman refuses to be anyone's victim.
~Maya Angelou~

191
To be a star, a diva, carries with it responsibility: one must learn to know and respect boundaries, using power in ways that enrich and uplift.
~bell hooks~

192
Having a positive attitude gives you the power to uplift, the power to create change, the power to motivate, the power to inspire, the power to influence, the power to cultivate happiness, and the list goes on.
~Lindsey Rietzsch~

193

If we are to remain mission focused, as we must if we are to be relevant in an uncertain age, then abandoning those things that do not further the mission is a leadership imperative.

~Frances Hesselbein~

INCLUSIVE LEADERSHIP

Leaders who are inclusive value the contributions of each member of the organization, institution, or community.

Inclusive leaders recognize the diversity in human systems and create a culture in which people of different backgrounds can use their skills, abilities, gifts, and experiences in service to the whole. Inclusive leaders work hard to not exclude members of the team based on stereotypes, biased perspectives, and unexamined assumptions. The inclusive leader sees the potential in others, and she develops others toward that potential. The inclusive leader has broken through barriers and now helps others break through barriers that separate and limit the potential, productivity, and power of the individual and the collective.

6

194

Feelings of worth can flourish only in an atmosphere where individual differences are appreciated, mistakes are tolerated, communication is open, and rules are flexible—the kind of atmosphere that is found in a nurturing family.
~Virginia Satir~

195

If they don't give you a seat at the table, bring a folding chair.
~Shirley Chisholm~

196

The only walls that exist are those you have placed in your mind. And whatever obstacles you conceive, exist only because you have forgotten what you have already achieved.
~Suzy Kassem~

197

I don't want my daughter to break any glass ceilings. I'd rather she never even contemplated their existence. Because glass ceilings, closed doors, and boy's clubs are notions, they're ideas, and they're not tangible. You can't see, touch, or feel them. They can only exercise power over us if we choose to believe in them. So why lay down your own gauntlet?
~Amy Mowafi~

198

This is the ultimate chicken and the egg situation. The chicken: Women will tear down the external barriers once we achieve leadership roles.... The egg: We need to eliminate the external barriers to get women into those roles in the first place. Both sides are right.
~Sheryl Sandberg~

199

Just as my mother said, "You can do anything if you put your mind to it, you work hard and you take that responsibility."
~Marillyn Hewson~

200

I do not wish them [women] to have power over men;
but over themselves.
~Mary Wollstonecraft~

201

You must make women count as much as men; you
must have an equal standard of morals; and the only
way to enforce that is through giving women political
power so that you can get that equal moral standard
registered in the laws of the country. It is the only way.
~Emmeline Pankhurst~

202

A strong woman is a woman determined to do
something others are determined not be done.
~Marge Piercy~

203

No country can ever truly flourish if it stifles the
potential of its women and deprives itself of the
contributions of half of its citizens.
~Michelle Obama~

204

I raise up my voice—not so I can shout, but so that those without a voice can be heard ... we cannot succeed when half of us are held back.
~*Malala Yousafzai*~

205

Tremendous amounts of talent are lost to our society just because that talent wears a skirt.
~*Shirley Chisholm*~

206

I believe that the rights of women and girls is the unfinished business of the twenty-first century.
~*Hillary Clinton*~

207

Leaders hoping to build diverse teams should be aware that in order to fully utilize the wider range of resources and increased learning that diversity offers, each member of the diverse group must be of equal status.
~*Dr. Christena Cleveland*~

208

The goals of reconciliation need to shift from
interpersonal acceptance to building reconciling
communities of racial, ethnic, class, and gender diversity.
~Dr. Brenda Salter-McNeil~

209

My dear fellow, who will let you? That's not the point.
The point is, who will stop me?
~Ayn Rand~

210

I'd like to see where boys and girls end up if they get
equal encouragement—I think we might have some
differences in how leadership is done.
~Sheryl Sandberg~

211

My argument is that getting rid of these internal barriers
is critical to gaining power. We can dismantle the hurdles
in ourselves today. We can start this very moment.
~Sheryl Sandberg~

212
In order to cultivate a set of leaders with legitimacy in the eyes of the citizenry, it is necessary that the path to leadership be visibly open to talented and qualified individuals of every race and ethnicity.
~Sandra Day O'Connor~

213
We should not be held back from pursuing our full talents, from contributing what we could contribute to the society, because we fit into a certain mold because we belong to a group that historically has been the object of discrimination.
~Ruth Bader Ginsburg~

214
When we believe in something, we got to stay with it, even when the world tells us no.
~Arianna Huffington~

215
I think the key is for women not to set any limits.
~Martina Navratilova~

216
Defining myself, as opposed to being defined by others, is one of the most difficult challenges I face.
~*Carol Moseley Braun*~

217
We need women at all levels, including the top, to change the dynamic, reshape the conversation, to make sure women's voices are heard and heeded, not overlooked and ignored.
~*Sheryl Sandberg*~

218
Never be limited by other people's limited imaginations.
~*Dr. Mae Jemison*~

219
Women are always saying, "We can do anything that men can do." But men should be saying, "We can do anything that women can do."
~*Gloria Steinem*~

220

We ask justice, we ask equality, we ask that all the civil and political rights that belong to citizens of the United States, be guaranteed to us and our daughters forever.
~Susan B. Anthony~

221

As leaders, we must go beyond simply naming and addressing our own biased perceptions or leading the members of our congregations and organizations in naming and addressing their biases. We must also take active steps to expand our category of us so that they are now included in us.
~Dr. Christena Cleveland~

222

Still, I wonder if more women artists, musicians, and writers aren't household names because we don't have enough faith in our own pursuits to give ourselves the time we desperately need to be transformed by a creative vision. Maybe that glass ceiling isn't really made of glass at all, but of sticky little fingers, dishes piled in the sink, and mortgages that demand two incomes.
~Holly Robinson~

223

Any society that fails to harness the energy and creativity of its women is at a huge disadvantage in the modern world.
~*Tian Wei*~

224

I think that no matter how smart, people usually see what they're already looking for.
~*Veronica Roth*~

225

I think the truth of the matter is, people who end up as "first" don't actually set out to be first. They set out to do something they love and it just so happens that they are the first to do it.
~*Condoleezza Rice*~

226

Ignore the glass ceiling and do your work. If you're focusing on the glass ceiling, focusing on what you don't have, focusing on the limitations, then you will be limited. My way was to work, make my short ... make my documentary... make my small films ... use my own money ... raise money myself ... and stay shooting and focused on each project.
~*Ava DuVernay*~

227
To achieve gender equality, we need to mobilise not just parliaments but populations, not only civil society, but all of society.
~Phumzile Mlambo-Ngcuka~

228
The history of all times, and of today especially, teaches that ... women will be forgotten if they forget to think about themselves.
~Louise Otto-Peters~

229
Create inclusion—with the simple mindfulness that others might have a different reality from your own.
~Patti Digh~

230
We needed to focus on creating an environment ... around diversity and inclusion. It starts with leadership. It really all starts with setting the tone at the top and having not only a vision about where you want to take the company from a standpoint of an inclusive environment, but also actionable, meaningful things you can do to make a difference on that.
~Marillyn Hewson~

231

Based on Catalyst research and my personal experience, I believe that humility, courage, and a willingness to disrupt the default are the traits most essential to successful leadership. Small moments can have a big impact on innovation, performance, and productivity.
~*Deborah Gillis*~

232

Of the many things I've learned during my first year as CEO, one of the most important is how crucial inclusive leadership is to enabling employees to do their best work.
~*Deborah Gillis*~

233

The real power of diversity ...[is] us women deciding to celebrate rather than apologize for all the amazing unique qualities that we bring to the table—and to give ourselves permission to act like our true selves at work.
~*Sallie Krawcheck*~

INTERACTIONAL LEADERSHIP

Leadership is not an event and is not limited to a title or role.

Leadership is an interactive process that is enhanced by how effective we communicate and collaborate with others for a common goal. Interactive leadership is about listening, building strong relational ties in service to a common purpose, and being ever aware of our mutual effect on one another.

7

234

Use each interaction to be the best, most powerful version of yourself.
~Marianne Williamson~

235

Solidarity between women can be a powerful force of change and can influence future development in ways favourable, not only to women but also to men.
~Nawal El Saadawi~

236

Every interaction is an opportunity to influence.
~Dr. Jeanne Porter King~

237

Communication. It's the first thing we learn in life. Funny thing is, once we grow up, learn our words and really start talking, the harder it becomes to know what to say. Or how to ask for what we really need.
~Dr. Meredith Grey~

238

Ninety percent of leadership is the ability to communicate something people want.
~Diane Feinstein~

239

Any time women come together with a collective intention, it's a powerful thing. Whether it's sitting down making a quilt, in a kitchen preparing a meal, in a club reading the same book, or around the table playing cards, or planning a birthday party, when women come together with a collective intention, magic happens.
~*Phylicia Rashad*~

240

With kids, they don't do what you want them to do when you want them to do it. Organizations don't necessarily, either. You've got to listen. You've got to learn how to influence.
~*Ellen Kullman*~

241

For good ideas and true innovation, you need human interaction, conflict, argument, debate.
~*Margaret Heffernan*~

242

My senior leadership team is half people who have been at GM for a long period of time like me, and others who have joined the company within the last five years from different industries, experiences, and countries. You have a better picture of the world. The diversity of thought is where you can make better business decisions.
~*Mary Barra*~

243

The first half of life is spent mainly in finding out who we are through seeing ourselves in our interaction with others.
~*June Singer*~

244

Treating people with kindness and respect seems elementary but is not always reciprocated. I often run into people who tell me a story about how I impacted their life—most often by an act of kindness that they never forgot.
~*April Uchitel*~

245

I realized I was more convincing to myself and to the people who were listening when I actually said what I thought, versus what I thought people wanted to hear me say.
~Ursula Burns~

246

In all interactions, from the smallest to the largest, the behavior of the "how to be" leader will demonstrate a belief in the worth and dignity of the men and women who make up the enterprise.
~Frances Hesselbein~

247

If you raise your hand, and you don't get called on, by the time you do, what you had to say doesn't make sense anymore. It's not germane. So I made up this term, *active listening*—you listen differently if you think you're going to interrupt.
~Madeline Albright~

248

The magic of influence is less in what we say and more in how we say it and who we are.
~Annette Simmons~

249

Intelligence, knowledge, or experience are important and might get you a job, but strong communication skills are what will get you promoted.
~*Mireille Guiliano*~

250

The real leadership lessons don't just come from official performance reviews and embarrassing setbacks. They also happen constantly in office hallways, around proverbial watercoolers, and, increasingly, online.
~*Sallie Ann Krawcheck*~

251

Women don't have to be defined by others. We have the power to define ourselves: by telling our own stories, in our own words, with our own voices.
~*Sarah Kay*~

252

Ce n'est pas la première fois que je remarque combine …
les mots ont plus d'empire que les idées.
(It's not the first time I've noticed how much more power words have than ideas.)
~*George Sand*~

253
One of the things that make people proud to work somewhere is having insights into how decisions are made.
~Marissa Mayer~

254
People follow a person who they feel "speaks the Truth."
~Annette Simmons~

255
I hope you will find some way to break the rules and make a little trouble out there. And I also hope that you will choose to make some of that trouble on behalf of women.
~Nora Ephron~

256
Women have to take responsibility for the dynamic around them. You can't just say, "Woe is me."
~Maggie Wilderotter~

257

One of the benchmarks of great communicators is their ability to listen not just to what's being said, but to what's not being said as well. They listen between the lines.
~Dr. Laurie Buchanan~

258

I prefer a naturalist style of conversation. Let's strip it down to what matters. Let's have emotions and beliefs on show without the modest covering of small talk.
~Rosamund Lupton~

259

If we don't communicate, we certainly can't get much done, and if we don't communicate authentically, what we get done is less effective.
~Michele Jennae~

260

Heartfelt communicators make such a difference in the lives of others through their authentic depth and sincere expression.
~Miya Yamanouchi~

261
I have a theory that sometimes people think they need to talk as much as possible, almost as if talking more equates to knowing more.
~Mary Mihalic~

262
People get really scared when women reclaim words, talk about themselves honestly and also make jokes because it's a really unstoppable combination.
~Caitlin Moran~

263
It is through relationships that we carve out our spheres of influence. Every person with whom we come into contact is influenced by us in one way or another.
~Dr. Cynthia Hale~

264
The things you say, the things you don't say, the things you do, or the things you don't do are always sending a loud message to those around you. What kind of a message are you sending? Is it a true reflection of who you are?
~Lindsey Rietzsch~

265

Women are still in emotional bondage as long as we need to worry that we might have to make a choice between being heard and being loved.
~*Marianne Williamson*~

266

It sometimes feels like the workplace is immune from social upheaval. We go to work and do the best we can, and at the end of the day, we return to our lives. We don't abandon who we are, however, when we begin and end our workday. Who we are shapes how we are perceived in the workplace and, in turn, how we perform in the workplace.
~*Roxane Gay*~

267

In this present culture, we need to find the means to work and live together with less aggression if we are to resolve the serious problems that afflict and impede us.
~*Margaret J. Wheatley*~

268

I need to listen well so that I hear what is not said.
~*Thuli Madonsela*~

269
You cannot shake hands with a clenched fist.
~Indira Gandhi~

270
Your own words are the bricks and mortar of the dreams you want to realize. Your words are the greatest power you have. The words you choose and their use establish the life you experience.
~Sonia Choquette~

271
If you have something worthwhile to contribute, don't hesitate to speak up. Presumably, you're there for a reason and it's not to decorate the office chairs.
~Madeline Albright~

272
Get specific sooner and reap many rewards. The specific detail or example proves the general conclusion, not the reverse. The more specific you are about anything the more clear you become, for yourself and in telling others. Thus, you reduce the chance of others misunderstanding you. And you become more compelling, credible, and memorable.
~Kare Anderson~

273

The art of civil conversation begins at birth. Then goes from the dinner table to the schoolroom, to interaction among friends, to the work place, and on to other places where all manner of social interactions are required.
~*Cindy Ann Peterson*~

274

Being able to look your coworkers in the eye when making a presentation, or being able to make eye contact with the audience when making a speech, has a transformative effect—on your ability to connect, to inspire, to create buy-in.
~*Sylvia Ann Hewlett*~

INTENTIONAL LEADERSHIP

Leadership must be purposeful, strategic.

In our fast-paced work, too many people try to lead on the fly or in the moment. This happenstance approach will provide accidental results. The effective leader is strategic, and every leader must learn to methodically and thoughtfully "aim" with intentionality to achieve goals and outcomes that benefit the organization, institution, and ultimately herself.

8

275

Intention is one of the most powerful forces there is. What you mean when you do a thing will always determine the outcome.
~Brenna Yovanoff~

276

You can't move so fast that you try to change the mores faster than people can accept it. That doesn't mean you do nothing, but it means that you do the things that need to be done according to priority.
~Eleanor Roosevelt~

277

Do not be afraid to make decisions. Do not be afraid to make mistakes.
~Carly Fiorina~

278

There are no overnight successes. It's a combination of humility, sacrifices, tenacity, failure, and opportunity.
~Timi Nadela~

279

My view to the stuff is always, "Oh, you think that? I'll show you. I'm going to work so hard. I'm going to be so on it, that my actions will speak for themselves and I don't have to say anything."
~Michelle Obama~

280

To stay ahead, you must have your next idea waiting in the wings.
~Rosabeth Moss Kanter~

281

The best way to ensure you achieve the greatest satisfaction out of life is to behave intentionally.
~Deborah Day~

282

I wake up every morning and think to myself, "How far can I push the company forward in the next twenty-four hours."
~Leah Busque~

283

The secret of getting ahead, is getting started.
~Sally Berger~

284
If you're not making mistakes, you're not making decisions.
~Catherine Cook~

285
A lot of people are afraid to say what they want. That's why they don't get what they want.
~Madonna~

286
Everything that has ever happened to me that has been important has not been something that I've hoped for, or looked for, or manipulated—it's all been predicated on my ability to take a new road when it presented itself and to go with it.
~Susan Sarandon~

287
To change any behavior, we have to slow down and act intentionally rather than from habit and impulse.
~Henna Inam~

288

First, give yourself permission to be a contrarian, to flout convention, to follow the unsafe path, to zig when everyone else zags; then, two, take some action to get going. Allow yourself to try; then try.
~Linda Rottenberg~

289

Most people just "hope" to meet their targets, while few have clear and strong intention hence they achieve it.
~Hina Hashmi~

290

Every action has an impact; choose wisely the impact you want to have.
~Dr. Mindy Hall~

291

If you don't give anything, don't expect anything. Success is not coming to you, you must come to it.
~Marva Collins~

292

My advice, having done this a number of times, is to go into an organization and figure out what that company's doing right, and do more of it. You'll eventually get to your to-do list and to your fix-it list, but if you come in and just talk about what's going wrong, you will lose hearts and minds.
~Meg Whitman~

293

Do the one thing you think you cannot do. Fail at it. Try again. Do better the second time. The only people who never tumble are those who never mount the high wire. This is your moment. Own it.
~Oprah Winfrey~

294

We are all gardeners, planting seeds of intention and watering them with attention in every moment of every day.
~Cristen Rodgers~

295

You need strategy to assume leadership, but only the character can sustain leaders as who they really are.
~Pearl Zhu~

296
If you can "hire tough," you can "manage easy."
~Sue Tetzlaff~

297
Define success on your own terms, achieve it by your own rules, and build a life you're proud to live.
~Anne Sweeney~

298
Instead of looking at the past, I put myself ahead twenty years and try to look at what I need to do now in order to get there then.
~Diana Ross~

299
Strategic leaders must not get consumed by the operational and tactical side of their work. They have a duty to find time to shape the future.
~Stephanie S. Mead~

300
The world's greatest achievers have been those who have always focused on their goals and have been consistent in their efforts.
~Dr. Roopleen~

301

When you accept a leadership role, you take on extra responsibility for your actions toward others.
~Kelley Armstrong~

302

Many of us are interested in talking about strategies for reconciliation, and that's good. But we need to realize that the most powerful ways we change are often out of our control. Change can be painful and coercive because we cannot control or manage it.
~Dr. Brenda Salter-McNeil~

303

Our power lies in our small daily choices, one after another, to create eternal ripples of a life well lived.
~Dr. Mollie Marti~

304

People who repeatedly find career success learn to broaden their perspective and understand that there are always several roads to getting where you want to go.
~Carla A. Harris~

305

Powerful words come with powerful intent. Where you have passion, strength, courage, and determination you can accomplish anything!
~K.L. Toth~

306

All great acts are ruled by intention. What you mean is what you get.
~Brenna Yovanoff~

307

Every action or perceived inaction shapes credibility.
~Dr. Mindy Hall~

308

I never dreamed about success. I worked for it.
~Estee Lauder~

309

The most effective way to do it is to do it.
~Amelia Earhart~

310

I am willing to put myself through anything; temporary pain or discomfort means nothing to me as long as I can see that the experience will take me to a new level. I am interested in the unknown, and the only path to the unknown is through breaking barriers, an often-painful process.

~Diana Nyad~

311

Life is not easy for any of us. But what of that? We must have perseverance and above all confidence in ourselves. We must believe that we are gifted for something, and that this thing, at whatever cost, must be attained.

~Marie Curie~

312

Yesterday it was all about getting in and today it is moving up.

~Bishop Vashti McKenzie~

313

When you disrupt yourself, you are looking for growth, so if you want to muscle up a curve, you have to push and pull against objects and barriers that would constrain and constrict you. That is how you get stronger.

~Whitney Johnson~

314

Where we choose to be, where we choose to be—we have the power to determine that in our lives. We cannot reel time backward or forward, but we can take ourselves to the place that defines our being.
~Sena Jeter Naslund~

315

Don't tell anyone your idea until you have invested enough of yourself in it that you are not going to turn back. When a person has an idea at that conception moment it is the most vulnerable—one negative comment could knock you off course.
~Sara Blakely~

316

One thing I know to be true: What we did yesterday won't get us through tomorrow. Leaders need to be forward-thinking, dynamic and insightful to drive value and deliver a competitive advantage.
~Kate Barton~

317

Purpose doesn't hurt margins. Purpose is how you drive transformation.
~Indra Nooyi~

318

I do not fix problems. I fix my thinking. Then
problems fix themselves.
~Lousie L. Hay~

319

Things change. We've gotten into the room. Now,
what will we do while we are there? We're at the table,
but will our voices be heard or will they be like voices
crying in the wilderness?
~Bishop Vashti McKenzie~

320

I have always believed you should have two strategies
when you're looking toward the future—you should
have the long-term strategy, which requires a lot of
discipline, but in the short term, you have to give
everyone the sense that there are changes going on
right now.
~Donna Shalala~

321

Others may be content with you watching the game
instead of playing the game because if you got in the
game you might just change the way the game is played.
~Bishop Vashti McKenzie~

CONNECTIVE LEADERSHIP

Leaders don't lead in isolation.

No leader, male or female, has gotten to a position of leadership without the help, support, and encouragement of others. Be they coaches, mentors, sponsors, promoters, connectors, cheerleaders, counselors, or friends, every effective leader exists within an infrastructure of supportive, connective people. In turn, those leaders commit to becoming a part of other existing and emerging leaders' networks of support.

9

322

If you are successful, it is because somewhere, sometime, someone gave you a life or an idea that started you in the right direction. Remember also, that you are indebted to life until you help some less fortunate person, just as you were helped.
~Melinda Gates~

323

Forget "six degrees of separation." Today it's "six degrees of CONNECTION."
~Morag Barrett~

324

Every Mary needs an Elizabeth (two, three, four Elizabeths!) who acts as a confidante, a friend, a partner, a mentor to help walk with her, especially along the bumpy parts of the journey, and if not all the way, for at least part of her journey.
~Dr. Renita Weems~

325

Our contribution is of no value unless it is effectively related to the contributions of all the others concerned.
~Mary Parker Follett~

326
Find the smartest people you can and surround
yourself with them.
~Marissa Mayer~

327
No person, trying to take responsibility for her or his
identity, should have to be so alone. There must be
those among whom we can sit down and weep, and
still be counted as warriors.
~Adrienne Rich~

328
There's something so quietly contained in the moments
when one reaches their hand out to support.... It's
hardly ever spoken about, but the feeling of belonging
to somewhere, or someone, for a split second gives
you enough power to carry on a few more steps. When
the world is full of compassionate people like this, the
world will know unconditional love.
~Nikki Rowe~

329
Encourage, lift, and strengthen one another. For the
positive energy spread to one will be felt by us all. For
we are connected, one and all.
~Deborah Day~

330
Stand up for the underdog, the "loser." Sometimes having the strength to show loving support for unacknowledged others turns the tides of our own lives.
~*Alexandra Katehakis*~

331
When a young person, even a gifted one, grows up without proximate living examples of what she may aspire to become … her goal remains abstract. Such models as appear in books or on the news, however inspiring or revered, are ultimately too remote to be real, let alone influential. But a role model in the flesh provides more than inspiration; his or her very existence is confirmation of possibilities one may have every reason to doubt, saying, "Yes, someone like me can do this."
~*Sonia Sotomayor*~

332
What kind of footsteps will you leave for those who follow you?
~*Kathy Bee*~

333
Wherever you find a great man, you will find a great mother or a great wife standing behind him—or so they used to say. It would be interesting to know how many great women have had great fathers and husbands behind them.
~Dorothy L. Sayers~

334
Once you've identified people who can be both mentors and sponsors, you need to make contact. Don't hesitate to introduce yourself to a potential ally at an event or in the elevator and say you admire her work.... You can also request an informational interview.
~Kate White~

335
But people need lift, too. People don't get moving, they don't soar, they don't achieve great heights, without someone buoying them up.
~Elizabeth Wein~

336
Be strong, be fearless, be beautiful. And believe that anything is possible when you have the right people there to support you.
~Misty Copeland~

337

If you need something from somebody, always give
that person a way to hand it to you.
~Sue Monk Kidd~

338

What I like about the mentoring relationship is that
it promotes creativity and collaboration. It may seem
like it's a one-way street, but believe me it's a two-way
street. Mentoring gives each of us a chance not only
to be a teacher, but also to be a student ... there is so
much we learn from each other.
~Hillary Clinton~

339

You all know that I have been sustained throughout
my life by three saving graces—my family, my friends,
and a faith in the power of resilience and hope. These
graces have carried me through difficult times and they
have brought more joy to the good times than I ever
could have imagined.
~Elizabeth Edwards~

340
One of the most critical decisions made in life is choosing with whom to spend your time. For it is those close relationships that gradually mold our character until we become a reflection of the company we keep.
~Richelle E. Goodrich~

341
If women are going to rise to the top, we need to start building supportive communities of high-achieving women and learn to ask for help from and give help to one another.
~Miereille Guiliano~

342
Women friends are not just a social act. They are a spiritual act.
~Sister Joan Chittister~

343
Women's friendships are like a renewable source of power.
~Jane Fonda~

344

It's time to get focused on what really matters. Find women that are different than you and figure out the things you have in common. We have a whole generation of girls who are looking at us to see how we treat each other. Let's show them what the power of being a woman really looks like. Let's open our arms to each other, and to them.
~Chelsea Handler~

345

I don't know what I would do without my women friends. They make me stronger. They make me smarter, they make me powerful. They tap me on the shoulder when I might be in need of course correcting.
~Jane Fonda~

346

Find a group of people who challenge and inspire you; spend a lot of time with them, and it will change your life.
~Amy Poehler~

347

I've seen how you can't learn anything when you're trying to be the smartest person in the room.
~Barbara Kingsolver~

348

A friend is someone who makes it easy to believe in yourself.

~Heidi Wills~

349

I have worked for a lot of really great leaders and mentors that I felt provided me, along with many of my peers—many of them women—opportunities.
~Mary T. Barra~

350

I've had many mentors, but the one that has the most impact was my mother.
~Ursula Burns~

351

I think the most important quality of a mentor is that they are open to following students where they want to go. Not always pushing their own agenda.
~Cordelia Jensen~

352

Today, the lines of mentoring and networking are blurring. Welcome to the world of mentworking.
~Julie Winkle Giulioni~

353

We should always have three friends in our lives—one who walks ahead who we look up to and follow; one who walks beside us, who is with us every step of our journey; and then, one who we reach back for and bring along after we've cleared the way.
~*Michelle Obama*~

354

What you really know in the end [is] that your relationships are what are most important. Those friendships, those people you love, the family members that you have—those are the relationships that I think also make a life well lived and make life so meaningful and valuable.
~*Laura Bush*~

355

The connections in and between women are the most feared, the most problematic, and the most potentially transforming force on the planet.
~*Adrienne Rich*~

356

Networks give you power. Your network is one of the most important competitive advantages you can have.
~*Carla A. Harris*~

357
The voices in the world have become increasingly diverse and interconnected.
~Dr. Cristena Cleveland~

358
To get that chance to lead, you need to know how to promote your own achievements to build a cadre of mentors and sponsors who will readily toss your name into the candidate pool for highly desirable fast-track positions.
~Jane Hyun~

359
Be someone's security blanket when theirs is in the wash.
~Richelle E. Goodrich~

360
As I look back over my mountains of growth and compare them to the molehills where I stagnated, community often made the difference.
~Mary E. DeMuth~

361

I believe I gather strength from the generations of women who came before me.
~Elizabeth Berrien~

362

You need mentors, sponsors, and coaches. The way I define those are coaches talk at you; mentors talk to you; and sponsors talk about you.
~Connie Lindsey~

363

In every critical decision about your career—promotions, compensation, important assignments—someone has to, as I like to say, "Carry your paper into the room."
~Carla A. Harris~

364

That day I learned that sometimes true victory is measured by with whom you finish the race, not how fast. Being supportive is more important than being impressive.
~Dr. Debbye Turner Bell~

365
There is nothing more beautiful than someone who goes out of their way to make life beautiful for others.
~Mandy Hale~

366
The sun still shines on the "Lone Ranger" leader, but her days are getting shorter.
~Bishop Vashti McKenzie~

ACKNOWLEDGMENTS

Special thanks to the women entrepreneurs and leaders that are critical parts of my "infrastructure of support."

Thank you, Gabriella Lindsay, for serving as a research assistant on this project. Your meticulous attention to detail and creativity in considering who counts as a leader has enriched this volume. Thanks to Debbye, Helen, Colette, and the Christ Community Church Women's Leadership Team for timely input. Our words matter; thank you for sharing yours with me.

Thanks to three of the best gifts in the creative industry: Jennifer LuVert of Forerunners Ink for copyediting and layout assistance; LaShaunn Tappler of LTComdesign for cover design, marketing, and publishing assistance; and Marina Woods of iMarketing PR for social media marketing.

BIOGRAPHIES

ADEN, HALIMA – Aden is a nineteen-year-old Somali-American who became the first contestant to compete wearing a hijab and later donned a burkini during the swimsuit portion of the evening in the Miss Minnesota USA pageant in November 2016.

AKITA, LAILAH GIFTY – Akita is the founder of Smart Youth Volunteers Foundation. A Ghanaian, she holds a doctorate in geosciences. She is a writer and passionate advocate for the empowerment of young people.

ALBRIGHT, MADELINE – Albright is a politician and diplomat and was the first woman to become the secretary of state as nominated by President Bill Clinton and sworn into office in 1997. She is the chair of the Albright Stonebridge Group and a professor of international relations at Georgetown. She received the Presidential Medal of Freedom by President Barack Obama in 2012.

ALDER, SHANNON L. – Alder is an inspirational author. Her quotes have been published in over 100 different books by various relationship authors and in several online magazine articles.

ALLEN, SHARON - Allen was the chairman of Deloitte & Touche in 2003. She has appeared on the *Forbes'* The World's 100 Most Powerful Women list multiple times and was the first woman to head one of the Big Four global accounting firms.

ANDERSON, GILLIAN LEIGH – Anderson is a television, film, and theater actress, activist, and writer. She is most widely known for her role as Agent Dana Scully on the popular series, *The X-Files*. In 2016, she was appointed as an honorary Officer of the Most Excellent Order of the British Empire for her services.

ANDERSON, KARE – Anderson is an Emmy-winning reporter and connective behavior speaker and columnist. She is currently a contributor for *Forbes* and *The Huffington Post*. She is a founding board member of Annie's Homegrown and an entrepreneur who runs her own speaking and consulting business.

ANGELOU, MAYA – Angelou was a memoirist, poet, and civil rights activist. She published three books of essays, seven autobiographies, several books of poetry along with numerous plays, movies, and television shows over a fifty-year span. She is the recipient of more than fifty honorary degrees, and she was awarded the Presidential Medal of Freedom in 2011.

ANTHONY, SUSAN B. – Anthony was a social reformer and women's rights activist who played a significant role in the women's suffrage movement. In 1856, she became the New York state agent for the American Anti-Slavery Society. Initially ridiculed for her views on women's rights and voting, in 1979 she became the first non-fictitious woman to appear on a US coin (the dollar coin).

ARMSTRONG, KELLEY – Armstrong is the author of twenty-one published books. She resides in Canada, where she focuses on writing fantasy novels and is well known for her *New York Times* best-sellers *No Humans Involved* and *The Awakening*.

ASH, MARY KAY – Ash was the founder of Mary Kay Cosmetics Inc. She received many honors from business groups and was inducted into the Junior Achievement U.S. Business Hall of Fame in 1996. Ash founded the Mary Kay Ash Charitable Foundation to raise money to combat cancer and domestic violence.

ATWOOD, MARGARET – Atwood is a Canadian poet, literary critic, essayist, novelist, and environmental activist. Many of her works speak to the conditions faced by women and the environment and examine current-day situations through the lens of the future. She is involved in humanitarian efforts, including being the honorary president of the Rare Bird Club of BirdLife International.

BAKER, ELLA – Baker was an African-American civil rights activist whose organizing career spanned over five decades. She is regarded as one of the most important African-American leaders of the twentieth century and one of the most influential women in the civil rights movement.

BARRA, MARY – Barra is the CEO and chairperson of General Motors. She was featured on the cover of *Time* magazine's The 100 Most Influential People in the World issue in April 2014. She has been with General Motors since 1980, starting out as an eighteen-year-old co-op student.

BARRETT, MORAG – Barrett is the CEO of SkyeTeam, an international HR consulting and leadership development company. She is a sought-out speaker who has trained over 3,000 leaders in twenty countries on four continents.

BARTON, KATE – Barton is a partner and vice chair of tax services at Ernst & Young LLP. She was recently named Female Executive of the Year by the Women World Awards for Women in Business in organizations with 2,500 or more employees.

BARTON, RUTH HALEY – Barton is the president and founder of the Transforming Center. She is also an author and an internationally recognized speaker on leadership and spirituality.

BEE, KATHY – Bee is a television producer, host, musical playwright, singer, songwriter, and the founder and CEO of PR Productions and Touching Lives Multimedia Inc. She has hosted over 250 television segments and was featured at the 2012 Touching Lives TV award show.

BELL, DEBBYE TURNER DR. – Dr. Turner Bell is an ordained minister, motivational speaker, veterinarian, talk show host, and winner of the 1990 Miss America pageant.

BELLINGER, PATRICIA – Bellinger is the executive director and adjunct lecturer at the Center for Public Leadership at the Harvard Kennedy School of Government. She has held important roles such as the group vice president of Global Diversity and Inclusion at BP in London.

BERGER, SALLY – Berger was the New York Museum of Modern Art (MoMA) film curator for thirty years.

BERRIEN, ELIZABETH – Berrien is the co-founder of the non-profit The Respite: A Centre for Grief & Hope, the founder of the organization Soul Widows, and a writer. She writes and speaks primarily about grief and loss and how to learn to live and cope with such.

BHATIA, HIMANSHU (SUE) – Bhatia is the CEO of Rose International Inc., one of the largest privately held companies in the St. Louis area. She specializes in consulting, IT, and professional services working with clients including AT&T, Verizon, and Chevron.

BLACKWELL, ELIZABETH – Blackwell, a British-born physician, was the first woman to receive a medical degree in the United States. She was a pioneer in the promotion of education of women in medicine in the U.S. and the United Kingdom.

BLAKELY, SARA – Blakeley is the founder of Spanx, which was founded in Atlanta, Georgia. In 2012, she was named in *Time* magazine's annual list of The 100 Most Influential People in the World. In 2014, *Forbes* named her the ninety-third most powerful woman in the world.

BONTA, VANNA – Bonta was an Italian-American actress, writer, and inventor. She is most famous for her novel *Flight: A Quantum Fiction Novel*. Much of her work focuses on space and space travel. Her invention was featured in *Sex in Space* in 2009 on the History Channel.

BRAUN, CAROL MOSELEY – Braun is a politician and lawyer who represented Illinois as senator from 1993 to 1999. She was the first female African American elected to the United States Senate. She currently runs a private law firm; she also launched a line of organic food products.

BROWN, BINTA NIAMBI – Brown is the founder of Big Mouth Records LLC, and she manages singer Grace Weber. A graduate of Columbia Law School, she has worked as a corporate lawyer for Craith, Swaine & Moore and Kirkland & Ellis, the latter of which she was a partner for seven years.

BUCHANAN, LAURIE DR. – Dr. Buchanan has been a holistic health practitioner and transformational life coach for the past fifteen years. She is an avid blogger and has authored books written with the intention of bridging the gap between where her clients are and where they want to be—body, mind, and spirit.

BURG, ANN E. – Burg is a writer and poet. She is best known for her work *All the Broken Pieces*. Her novels have won awards and designations. She writes predominately in the young adult and children's genres.

BURNS, URSULA – Burns is the chairman of Xerox. She served as the company's CEO from 2009 to 2016. The first black woman to head a Fortune 500 company, she was rated the twenty-second among *Forbes*'s The 100 Most Powerful Woman in the World in 2014.

BUSQUE, LEAH – Busque founded TaskRabbit, which is an online and mobile marketplace that allows users to outsource small jobs and tasks to others in their area. She has coined the term, "service networking."

BUSH, LAURA – Bush is a former First Lady married to George W. Bush, the forty-third president of the United States. She is an advocate for literacy and education, causes she took on during her husband's administration. She collaborated with the Library of Congress to start the National Book Festival in Washington, D.C., which continues today.

CARTER, ROSALYNN – Carter is the wife of Jimmy Carter, who served as the thirty-ninth president of the United States. She is widely known for being a leading advocate for mental health research. She is the president of the board of directors for the Rosalynn Carter Institute for Caregiving.

CHER (CHERLYN SARKISIAN) – Cher is well known for her distinctive contralto singing voice. She has recorded numerous award-winning albums and has starred in many movies and television programs. She is a social activist who has championed several causes, including civil rights and HIV/AIDS prevention.

CHISHOLM, SHIRLEY ANITA ST. HILL – Chisholm was an American politician, author, and educator. She was the first African-American woman elected to the United States Congress, representing New York's Twelfth Congressional District. She held the position for seven terms from 1969 to 1983. She was the first black and first woman candidate for a major party's nomination for president of the United States (Democratic, 1972).

CHITTISTER, SIS. JOAN – Chittister is a Benedictine nun, author, and international speaker. She holds many advanced degrees. She speaks and writes on the topics of peace, spirituality, religious life, and justice. She has written over fifty books and over 700 articles.

CHOQUETTE, SONIA – Choquette is an author, spiritual teacher, and storyteller. She is the author of nineteen internationally best-selling books centered on awakening, personal growth, and creative growth.

CICCONE, MADONNA – Madonna is a singer, songwriter, businesswoman, and actress. She has often been referred to as the "Queen of Pop." She released her debut album in 1983 and has been performing ever since. She is the highest grossing female touring artist of all times.

CLARK, MARSHA – Clark is the principal of Marsha Clark and Associates, a change management and executive coaching firm that specializes in developing women leaders. Before launching her own firm, Marsha held a number of executive roles for Electronic Data Systems (EDS).

CLARKE, MONIF – Clarke is a leading designer of clothing for plus-size women and the co-founder (along with her mother) of Monif C. Plus Sizes. She is being recognized as one of the first to bring high fashion to plus-size apparel. She has a business background and earned a degree in mathematics and computer science from Rutgers University.

CLEVELAND, CRISTENA DR. – DR. Cleveland is a social psychologist, public theologian, author, and professor. She is an award-winning researcher and gifted teacher who brings organizational experience to her efforts to build unity. She consults with pastors and organizational leaders on multicultural issues and speaks regularly at organizations, churches, conferences, universities, and schools.

CLINTON, HILLARY – Clinton is an American politician who held the titles of United States secretary of state (2009-2013), New York senator (2001-2009), and First Lady of the United States (1999-2001). In 2016, she was the Democratic Party's nominee for president of the United States.

COLE, JOHNETTA B. DR. – Dr. Cole was the first African-American female president of Spellman College, serving the historically black college for women from 1987 to 1997. An anthropologist, she is the current director of the Smithsonian National Museum of African Art.

COLLINS, MARVA – Collins was an educator who started the Westside Preparatory School to encourage education among the youth of Chicago's Garfield Park neighborhood in 1975. She ran the school along with her daughter for more than thirty years.

COLLINS, PATRICIA HILL – Collins is a distinguished university professor at the University of Maryland. She is a past president of the American Sociological Association Council. She is an award-winning scholar on gender.

COOK, CATHERINE – Cook founded a social networking service called myYearbook (now MeetMe) in 2005 as a sophomore in high school.

JOY COOPER – Cooper is an award-winning American artist who began painting seriously in 1995. Based in West Virginia, her work has been exhibited in state and local art shows. She is a member of the West Virginia Watercolor Society and Allied Artists of West Virginia.

COPELAND, MISTY – Copeland is an American ballet dancer who became the first African-American woman to be promoted to principal dancer at the American Ballet Theater. She has won numerous awards, been featured in many ads, and has appeared on television and Broadway.

CRENSHAW, KIMBERLE WILLIAMS – Crenshaw is a civil rights advocate and leading scholar in the critical race theory field. She is a full professor at the UCLA School of Law and Columbia Law School. She specializes in race and gender issues and is known for the introduction and development of intersectional theory.

CUDDY, AMY – Cuddy is a social psychologist, author, and lecturer. She is best known for her research on emotion, power, nonverbal behavior, stereotyping, and discrimination and the effects of social stimuli on hormone levels. She is an associate professor of business administration at the Harvard Business School.

CURIE, MARIE – Curie was a Polish-French chemist and physicist who was a pioneer in radioactivity research. She was the first woman to win the Nobel Peace Prize and the first person and woman to win it twice, in two different sciences. She developed and coined the term "radioactivity."

DAVENPORT, BARRIE – Davenport is a coach, blogger, and online teacher. She writes books focused on topics such as relationships, building confidence, positive habits, mindfulness, and improved emotional intelligence.

DAY, DEBORAH – Day is a clinician in the mental health field. She offers coaching services, workshops, and trainings, and she hosts a twelve-week empowerment group for women.

DEARMAN, NANCY – Dearman is a founding member and owner of Kotter International, an organizational transformation firm grounded in the leadership principles of John Kotter.

DEMUTH, MARY E. – DeMuth is a writer and speaker who is passionate about encouraging others to change their lives. She is the author of twelve books and speaks around the country.

DEW, SHERI LINN – Dew is an author, publisher, and president and CEO of the Deseret Book Company. She has served as a religious leader in the Church of Jesus Christ of Latter-day Saints and an inspirational speaker.

DIGH, PATTI – Digh is an author, speaker, community builder, educator, and activist. She is the author of eight books and has been published in over 100 articles across notable international publications. She is an award-winning blogger.

DRESSER, DENISE DR. – Dr. Dresser is a political analyst, writer, and professor. *Forbes* named her as one of Mexico's most powerful women and one of the fifty most influential women on Twitter. She currently teaches in the political science department at the Instituto Technológico Autónomo de México (ITAM).

DUVERNAY, AVA MARIE – DuVernay is a director, screenwriter, film executive best known for her film *Selma*. She was the first black female director to be nominated for a Golden Globe Award and an Academy Award for Best Picture.

EARHART, AMELIA – Earhart was an author and aviation pioneer. She was the first female aviator to fly solo across the Atlantic Ocean. She set many records, received numerous awards, and wrote multiple best-selling books.

EDELMAN, MARIAN WRIGHT – Edelman is an activist for the rights of children. She is the president and founder of the Children's Defense Fund. She has been a lifelong advocate for disadvantaged Americans.

EDWARDS, ELIZABETH – Edwards was an attorney, best-selling author, health-care activist, and the wife of former U.S. senator John Edwards. She served as her husband's chief policy attorney during his presidential bid. She wrote two books, both best-sellers.

EL SAADAWI, NAWAL – El Saadawi is a physician, psychiatrist, writer, activist, and feminist who has written many books on the subject of women in Islam, focusing particularly on the practice of female genital mutilation. She has held many important positions and founded many organizations, including the Arab Women's Solidarity Association.

ELIOT, GEORGE – Eliot (Mary Ann Evans) was an English novelist, journalist, translator, poet, and one of the leading writers of the Victorian era. She has authored seven novels.

EPHRON, NORA – Ephron was a journalist, novelist, director, blogger, and producer best known for her romantic comedies. She was nominated for Academy Awards for her writing in *Silkwood*, *When Harry Met Sally*, and *Sleepless in Seattle*.

FARREL, PAM – Farrel is an international speaker, relationship specialist, and author of over twenty-five books. She is the president of Seasoned Sisters and frequently makes guest appearances on programs such as *Focus on the Family*.

FEINSTEIN, DIANE – Feinstein is the senior senator from California (Democratic Party). She has been a member of the senate since 1992 and previously served as the thirty-eighth mayor of San Francisco.

FEY, TINA – Fey is a comedian, actress, and writer best known for her work on *Saturday Night Live*. She has also written and co-starred in the series *30 Rock* and *Unbreakable Kimmy Schmidt*.

FIORINA, CARLY – Fiorina was the CEO of Hewlett-Packard from 1999 to 2005. She was the first woman to lead a top-twenty company as ranked by *Fortune* magazine.

FOLLETT, MARY PARKER – Follett was an early twentieth-century political scientist whose groundbreaking ideas on leadership served as the basis for participative management, collaborative leadership, and managing conflict. She conceptualized the idea of "power-with" as an alternative to "power-over."

FONDA, JANE – Fonda is an actress, writer, fashion model, and fitness guru. She is a two-time Academy-Award winner and two-time BAFTA-Award winner. She is also a visible political activist and co-founder of the Women's Media Center.

FRANK, ANNE – Frank is the author of *Anne Frank: The Diary of a Young Girl*, which is one of the world's most widely known books. She and her family hid in some concealed rooms behind a bookcase during

Nazi control over Germany. She and her family were discovered, sent to the Bergen-Belsen concentration camp in Auschwitz, where Frank died.

FULENWIDER, ANNE – Fulenwider is editor-in-chief of *Marie Claire* magazine. Married to a branding and media strategist, she lives in Brooklyn with her husband and two children.

FULLER, MARGARET – Fuller was a critic, journalist, and women's rights advocate. She was the first full-time American female book reviewer in journalism. Her book, *Woman in the Nineteenth Century,* is considered the first major feminist work in the U.S.

GANDHI, INDIRA – Gandhi was an Indian politician and prominent figure in the Indian National Congress. She was also the only female prime minister of India (1966-1977 and 1980-1984). In 1999, she was posthumously named Woman of the Millennium in a BBC poll.

GATES, MELINDA – Gates is a businesswoman and philanthropist, Gates is co-founder of the Bill & Melinda Gates Foundation. In 2016, she and her husband, Bill Gates, were honored with the Presidential Medal of Freedom for their philanthropic works by President Barack Obama.

GAY, ROXANE – Gay is an associate professor of English at Purdue University, contributing opinion writer at *The New York Times,* founder of Tiny Hardcore Press, co-editor of PANK, and the essays editor for The Rumpus. She authored the best-seller *Bad Feminist,* a collection of essays on "how to be human."

GIBBS, NANCY – Gibbs is an essayist and managing editor for *Time* magazine. She has multiple *New York Times* best-sellers and is a commentator on politics and values in the United States.

GILLIS, DEBORAH – Gillis is president and CEO of Catalyst. Catalyst is a leading nonprofit organization with a mission to accelerate progress for women through workplace inclusion.

GINSBURG, RUTH BADER – Ginsburg is an associate justice of the Supreme Court of the United States, appointed by President Bill Clinton in 1993. She is the second woman appointed to such a position.

GIULIONI, JULIE WINKLE – Giulioni is the co-founder and principal of DesignArounds, a multi-disciplinary team that creates award-winning electronic and instructor-led training. She is a well-respected author and speaker. She has been in the field for over twenty-five years and has worked with hundreds of organizations.

GOLDBERG, WHOOPI – Goldberg is a comedian, actress, author, and television host. She has been nominated for numerous awards and holds an Emmy, a Grammy, an Oscar, and a Tony Award. She was the second black woman in the history of the Academy Awards to win an acting Oscar.

GOODRICH, RICHELLE – Goodrich is a writer whose work has been published in a number of books, including *Chicken Soup for the Soul: Christmas in Canada*.

GREY, MEREDITH DR. – Dr. Meredith Grey is a fictional character on the popular television drama *Grey's Anatomy*, created by Shonda Rhimes.

GUILIANO, MIREILLE – Guiliano is the former president and CEO of Clicquot Inc. and spokesperson for Champagne Veuve Clicquot. She has been dubbed the "high priestess of French lady wisdom." She is the best-selling author of *French Women Don't Get Fat: The Secret of Eating for Pleasure*.

HALE, CYNTHIA DR. – Dr. Cynthia L. Hale is the founding and senior pastor of the Ray of Hope Christian Church in Decatur, Georgia. Ray of Hope has an active membership of 5,000 members. She was selected by then Senator Barack Obama and the Democratic Party to give the opening invocation at the 2008 Democratic National Convention. She also served as co-chair for "Women in Ministry" for former president Obama.

HALE, MANDY – Hale is a blogger and author who inspires single women to live their best lives and to never settle. She has been featured in various magazines and journals, most notably *Forbes*, *The Huffington Post*, and *Nashville Lifestyles*.

HALL, MINDY DR. – Dr. Hall is an author and the president and CEO of Peak Development Consulting LLC. She has worked worldwide helping companies create sustainable organization and leadership development solutions.

HANDLER, CHELSEA – Handler is a comedian, writer, actress, television host, and producer. In 2012, *Time* recognized her as one of The 100 Most Influential People. She was the host of the late-night talk show *Chelsea Lately* and has since performed and appeared in many other programs and sitcoms.

HARRIS, CARLA A. – Harris is vice chairman of wealth management, a managing director, and senior client advisor at Morgan Stanley. In 2013, she was appointed to chair the National Women's Business Council by President Barack Obama. She has been recognized with many awards and honors.

HASHMI, HINA – Hashmi is a intuitive empowerment and happiness coach, migraine cure specialist, international speaker, and clinical psychologist. She has been featured on television and radio and has written numerous guest blogs.

HAY, LOUISE L. – Hay is an author, speaker, soulful teacher, healer, and artist. She has written many books, including *The New York Times* best-selling book *You Can Heal Your Life*. She is a successful businesswoman and advocate.

HEFFERNAN, MARGARET – Heffernan is a businesswoman, interviewer, author, and TED speaker. She is the author of five books and can often be found encouraging others to take little at face value and regularly question received wisdom.

HEIGHT, DOROTHY DR. – Dr. Height was an administrator and educator and a civil and women's rights activist. She was the president of the National council of Negro Women for forty years and received the Presidential Medal of Freedom in 1994 and the Congressional Gold Medal in 2004. Holding many positions of influence throughout her lifetime, she was an honored guest at the 2009 inauguration of Barack Obama, the forty-fourth president of the United States.

HEPBURN, AUDREY – Hepburn was a British actress, model, dancer, and humanitarian. She won Academy, Emmy, Grammy and Tony awards. Later in life, she devoted much of her time to UNICEF.

HESSELBEIN, FRANCES – Hesselbein is the president and CEO of the Frances Hesselbein Leadership Institute. She served as the CEO for the Girl Scouts of the USA from 1976 to 1990 and was awarded the Presidential Medal of Freedom in 1998.

HEWLETT, SYLVIA ANN – Hewlett is an economist, author, and speaker who founded the Center for Talent Innovation and Hewlett Consulting Partners LLC. Experienced in global talent management, she focuses on the "power of difference" and the challenges unique to women and previously excluded groups.

HEWSON, MARILLYN – Hewson is the chairwoman and CEO of Lockheed Martin. She was named the twentieth most powerful woman in the world by *Forbes* magazine. She has been with Lockheed Martin since 1983.

HOOKS, BELL – Neé Gloria Jean Watkins, bell hooks is a prolific African-American author, feminist, and social activist.

HUFFINGTON, ARIANNA – Huffington is a Greek-American businesswoman, syndicated columnist, and author. She was the co-founder and editor-in-chief of *The Huffington Post*. She has since stepped down to devote time to her newest endeavor, Thrive Global focused on health and wellness information.

HYUN, JANE – Hyun is the founder and president of Hyun and Associates and serves as an executive coach and global leadership strategist. Author of the groundbreaking book *Breaking the Bamboo Ceiling*, she works with organizations to develop strategies for breaking through.

INAM, HENNA – Inam is the CEO of Transformational Leadership. A graduate of the Wharton School, she has worked with Fortune 500 companies as well as the Harvard Business School.

JEMISON, MAE CAROL DR. – Dr. Jemison is an engineer, physician, and NASA astronaut. She was the first African-American woman to travel into space in 1992. She is a dancer and actress and holds nine honorary doctorates in science, engineering, and more. She is the principal of the 100 Year Starship organization.

JENNAE, MICHELE – Jennae is a coach and consultant for companies and individuals. She is involved with numerous networking groups and chambers of commerce.

JENSEN, CORDELIA – Jensen is a writer of numerous young adult novels. She is a writer in residence at Big Blue Marble Bookstore, where she teaches creative writing and conducts author interviews. Jensen was the Poet Laureate of Perry County (2006-2007).

JOHNSON, ABIGAIL PIERREPONT – Johnson is the president and CEO of the American investment firm Fidelity Investments and the chairwoman of its international sister company, Fidelity International. Her wealth of approximately $14 billion makes her one of the world's wealthiest women.

JOHNSON, WHITNEY – Johnson is a regular contributor to the Harvard Business Review. She co-founded the Forty Women over Forty to Watch and was named by *Fortune* as one of The 55 Most Influential Women on Twitter in 2014. She is a speaker, writer, thought leader, and innovator.

JONES-DEWEEVER, AVIS A. DR. – Dr. Jones-Deweever is a career reinvention strategist, diversity consultant, and women's empowerment expert. She formerly served as the youngest ever executive director of the National Council of Negro Women.

JUSTICE, VICTORIA – Justice is an American singer and actress. She is well known for many project collaborations with Nickelodeon. Her charitable works include working with children's hospitals.

KANTER, ROSABETH MOSS – Kanter is a professor at Harvard Business School. She is the chair and director of the Harvard University Advanced Leadership Initiative, where she specializes in innovation, strategy, and leadership for change.

KASSEM, SUZY – Kassem is a filmmaker, philosopher, cultural critic, essayist, poet, and author. Her first book, *Rise Up and Salute the Sun,* is a cult classic that has garnered attention from readers in the United States and Egypt. Her work has been recognized by *Publisher's Weekly.*

KATEHAKIS, ALEXANDRA – Katehakis is the founder and clinical director of the Center for Healthy Sex. She has written numerous books and co-authored a daily meditation book, *Mirror of Intimacy,* which has garnered several awards. She is a regular contributor to *The Huffington Post* and *Psychology Today.*

KAY, SARAH – Kay (Sera) is an American poet known for her spoken word poetry. She is the founder and co-director of Projector VOICE (2004), an organization dedicated to using spoken word as an educational and inspirational tool.

KELLER, HELEN – An author, political activist, and lecturer, Helen Keller was the first deaf and blind person to receive a bachelor's degree. Her story has been widely told through various depictions of the play and film *The Miracle Worker*, about her relationship with Anne Sullivan.

KIDD, SUE MONK – Kidd is an American writer popularly known for her 2002 book, *The Secret Life of Bees*. She has written numerous novels that have been featured on *The New York Times* best-sellers list. She has also written memoirs and appeared on OWN.

KING, CORETTA SCOTT – King was an American civil rights activist, international human rights champion, author, the wife of Rev. Dr. Martin Luther King Jr., and mother of four.

KING, JEANNE PORTER DR. – Dr. Porter King is an author, consultant, and inspirational speaker. She is the founder and president of the TransPorter Group Inc., a practice that specializes in leadership development. She is the compiler of this volume of quotes.

KINGSOLVER, BARBARA – Kingsolver is an essayist, novelist, and poet. Each book she has written since 1992 has been placed on *The New York Times* best-seller's list. She was nominated for the Pulitzer Prize. In 2000, Kingsolver established the Bellwether Prize, which is designed to support literature that works for social change.

KNOWLES-CARTER, BEYONCÉ – Knowles-Carter is a songwriter, singer, and actress. She got her start in the all-female R&B group Destiny's Child and has since built an epic solo career. She has won five Grammys.

KOCHHAR, CHANDA – Kochhar is the managing director and CEO of ICICI Bank. She has radically changed retail banking in India. She has won many awards and received many accolades, and she has consistently maintained her place in *Fortune*'s and *Forbes*'s most powerful women lists.

KRAWCHECK, SALLIE – Krawcheck is the founder and CEO of Ellevest, an online investment company designed with and for women. Before starting her own company, she was president of the Global Wealth & Investment Management division of Bank of America.

KUBLER-ROSS, ELISABETH – Kubler-Ross was a psychiatrist and pioneer in near-death studies. In 2007, she was inducted into the American National Women's Hall of Fame. She was the recipient of twenty honorary degrees and was the preeminent speaker on the topics of death and dying.

KULLMAN, ELLEN – Kullman was the chair and CEO of DuPont and former director of General Motors. In 2014, *Forbes* ranked her thirty-first among its The 100 Most Powerful Women list.

LAUDER, ESTEE – Lauder was a businesswoman and co-founder of Estee Lauder Companies, known for cosmetics. In 1998 she was the only woman listed on *Time* magazine's The 20 Most Influential Business Geniuses of the 20th Century. She also received the Presidential Medal of Freedom in 1988.

LEWIN, LESLIE – Lewin is the executive director of Seeds for Peace.

LIGHT, JUDITH – Light is a two-time Tony-Award winning actress and producer. She has performed on television, in movies, and on Broadway. She is an activist who has launched many projects, including the True Colors Fund.

LINDSAY, GABRIELLA, M. – Lindsay worked as research assistant on *That's What She said! 366 Leadership Quotes by Women*. She is an author, blogger, freelance writer, and women's empowerment advocate. She recently published her first book, *Living F.I.T.: A 40-Day Guide to Living Faithfully, Intentionally, and Tenaciously*. Lindsay is a wife, mother of three, and a former elementary school teacher and administrator.

LINDSEY, CONNIE – Lindsey is the EVP and head of corporate social responsibility and global diversity and inclusion for Northern Trust, a wealth management institution based in Chicago. She is also a past president of *National Board of Girl Scouts of the USA.*

LIVELY, BLAKE – Lively is an actress most notably recognized for her role on *Gossip Girl.* She has appeared in various other television programs and movies, most recently *The Shallows.*

LOPEZ, JENNIFER – Lopez is a singer, dancer, designer, businesswoman, producer, and author. She was the first Latina actress to earn over $1 million for a film (*Out of Sight*). She is regarded as the most influential Hispanic performer in the U.S. She is also the highest paid Latina actress in the U.S. She owns a clothing line, a production company and a charitable foundation, among other things.

LORDE, AUDRE – Lorde was a writer, feminist, womanist, poet, and civil rights activist. She often used her poetry to speak to the conditions of women and people of color and to express her anger and outrage at civil and social injustices observed throughout her life. She was named the New York State Poet Laureate in 1991.

LUPTON, ROSAMUND – Lupton is a British author best known for her novels *Sister* and *Afterwards.* Her books have been featured on *The New York Times* best-sellers list.

MADONSELA, THULI – Madonsela (Thulisile Nomkhosi), who served as the public protector of South Africa from 2009 to 2016, is a South African advocate who helped draft the final constitution of South Africa promulgated by then president Nelson Mandela. In 2016, she was chosen as one of BBC's 100 Women.

MARTI, MOLLIE DR. – Marti is an adjunct professor of psychology at University of Iowa, a licensed psychologist, and a lawyer. She has written many books and runs a nonprofit organization, the *Community*

Resiliency Project, which helps communities recover from crises and grow their capacity to handle challenges.

MARCUS, BONNIE – Marcus is an award-winning entrepreneur and a *Forbes* and *Business Insider* contributing writer who helps professional women navigate the workplace to position themselves to advance their careers. She consults with companies to retain and support their female talent.

MAYER, MARISSA – Mayer is an information technology executive and currently serves as the CEO of Yahoo. She is a longtime executive, usability leader, and key spokesperson for Google.

MEAD, STEPHANIE S. – Mead is the current senior vice president of CMOE. Her work centers on operations management, leadership and employee development, organization effectiveness, consulting, and curriculum design.

MEARS, HENRIETTA – Mears was a Christian educator, evangelist, author, and one of the founders of the National Sunday School Association. She is the director of Christian education at First Presbyterian Church of Hollywood, California.

MCCARTHY, WENDY – McCarthy is an Australian businesswoman and in 2013 served as the director of the Australia's Top 100 Women of Influence.

MCKENZIE, VASHTI MURPHY – McKenzie is the bishop of the Tenth Episcopal District of the African Methodist Episcopal Church. She was the first female elected as bishop in the denomination's history. She is also the national chaplain of the Delta Sigma Theta Sorority Incorporated.

MIHALIC, MARY – Mihalic is the author of *Made to Make It* and other works. She navigates the business world and is a rising star in the corporate world.

MIRACLE, KATHERINE – Miracle is a thought leader, expert marketer, revenue development strategist, and motivator, among many other things. She is the founder and owner of Miracle Resources, a full-service marketing and training firm. She has written three books.

MLAMBO-NGCUKA, PHUMZILE – Mlambo-Ngcuka is the under-secretary-general of the United Nations and executive director of UN Women. Born in South Africa, she has been active in government and civil work for much of her life and has devoted her career to fighting for human rights, equality, and social justice.

MONTGOMERY, LUCY MAUD – Montgomery was a Canadian author best known for *Anne of Green Gables*. She has published over twenty novels, 530 short stories, 500 poems, and thirty essays. She was made an officer of the Order of the British Empire in 1935.

MORAN, CAITLIN – Moran is a journalist, broadcaster, and author. She writes three columns a week for *The Times*, a British news publication. She was named Columnist of the Year by the London Press Club in 2012, among other prestigious honors and awards she has received.

MOWAFI, AMY – Mowafi is the Egyptian-born co-founder of MO4, which is known for delivering e-content, web development, and social media management. She is a writer, and her books *FeMail* and *FeMail 2* have been popular among Egyptian youth.

MYERS, DEE DEE – Myers is a political analyst who served as the White House press secretary during the first two years of the Clinton administration. She was the first woman and second youngest person to hold the position. Myers co-hosted the news program *Equal Time* on CNBC.

NADELA, TIMI – Nadela is an author, entrepreneur, and speaker. She works directly with small business owners. She also serves as a life coach.

NASLUND, SENA JETER – Naslund is a *New York Times* notable author. She is the program director for the MFA in Writing at Spaulding University and a writer-in-residence at the University of Louisville. In 2005, she was named Poet Laureate of Kentucky.

NAVRATILOVA, MARTINA – Navratilova is a retired Czech and American tennis player who was named as the greatest female tennis player for the years 1965-2005. She has won innumerable awards, including a record-setting nine Wimbledon titles (six of which were consecutive).

NAYLOR, GLORIA – Naylor was an award-winning novelist best known for her groundbreaking writing. Her novels include *The Women of Brewster Place*, *Mama Day*, *Linden Hills*, and *Baily's Café*.

NAZARIAN, VERA – Nazarian is a speculative fiction writer. Her works have won many distinctions and awards. Her novel, *The Mists of Avalon*, was made into a TNT original mini-series.

NOOYI, INDRA (KRISHNAMURTHY) – Nooyi is the current chairperson and CEO of PepsiCo. She has been ranked among the world's 100 most powerful women in both *Forbes* and *Fortune* magazines.

NYAD, DIANA – Nyad is a long-distance swimmer, journalist, motivational speaker, and journalist. At the age of 64, she was the first woman to swim from Cuba to Florida without a shark cage.

OBAMA, MICHELLE LAVAUGHN ROBINSON – Obama is a writer, lawyer, and former First Lady. She is married to Barack Obama, the forty-fourth president of the United States. She is a graduate of Princeton University and Harvard Law School.

O'CONNOR, SANDRA DAY – O'Connor is a retired associate justice of the Supreme Court of the United States (1981-2006). She was the first woman to serve as a Justice of the U.S. Supreme Court.

OSTEEN, VICTORIA – Osteen is co-pastor of Lakewood Church in Houston, Texas. She is an author, speaker, and is married to Joel Osteen.

OTTO-PETERS, LOUISE – Otto-Peters was a writer, feminist, and social activist who championed the causes of women. She is known for starting the organized German women's movement.

PANKHURST, EMMELINE – Pankhurst was a British political activist and leader of the British suffragette movement. She was named as one of The 100 Most Important People of the 20th Century by *Time* magazine in 1999.

PARKS, ROSA – Parks was a civil rights activist. She is most notably recognized for refusing to give up her seat for a white passenger on a bus in Montgomery, Alabama, on December 1, 1955, sparking the Montgomery bus boycott.

PARTON, DOLLY – Parton is a singer, songwriter, instrumentalist, actress, record producer, author, and philanthropist. She is the most honored female country performer of all time. Parton has been nominated for forty-six Grammys.

PETERSON, CINDY ANN – Peterson is a designer, author, international keynote, style editor, and trainer. She has received numerous awards for her unique views on image transformation, fashion, and education and has a broad base of clientele from government to industry and academia.

PELOSI, NANCY – Pelosi is the Minority Leader of the House of Representatives representing California's Twelfth Congressional District. Formerly, she served as the Speaker of the House of Representatives from 2007 to 2011. She was the only woman to hold such an office, and to date she is the highest-ranking female politician in American history.

PIERCY, MARGE – Piercy is a writer and poet. She writes about women's rights and empowerment and together with her husband is the founder of Leapfrog Press, a small literary publishing company.

POEHLER, AMY – Poehler is a director, producer, actress, voice artist, writer, and comedian. She was a cast member of the popular program *Saturday Night Live* from 2001 to 2008. She has been nominated for eighteen Emmy Awards and in 2016 won the Primetime Emmy Award for Outstanding Guest Actress in a Comedy Series (SNL).

POOLE, MARY D. – Poole is a teacher of history at Prescott College. She has served as an analyst with the Washington State Senate, where she was responsible for drafting budgets for state and federal welfare programs.

POTTER, BEATRIX – Potter (Helen) was an English writer, illustrator, natural scientist, and conservationist who was best known for her children's books, such as *The Tale of Peter Rabbit*. She is the author of over thirty books, twenty-four of them children's tales.

PRATT, CHARLEYSE DR. – Dr. Pratt served as an executive for Cleveland State University. Dr. Pratt also was the founding director of CSU's Sullivan-Deckard Scholars Opportunity Program, which provides scholarships for students who have aged out of the foster care system. The program has its home in The Pratt Center, named in honor of Dr. Pratt.

PRIESAND, RABBI SALLY – Rabbi Priesand is the first female rabbi ordained by a rabbinical seminary and the second formally ordained female rabbi in Jewish history (1972). She spent thirty-five years in the rabbinate. Priesand is the author of several books. She has also been featured in numerous books and is the recipient of multiple awards and honors.

QUEEN ELIZABETH II – Queen Elizabeth II has been Queen of the United Kingdom, Australia, New Zealand, and Canada since 1952. She is also Head of the Commonwealth. She is a popular queen, and support of her monarchy is high.

RAE, KATIE – Rae is the managing director of Techstars Boston and founder of Project 11, a firm that assists start-ups.

RAND, AYN – Rand was a philosopher, playwright, screenwriter, and novelist best known for her best-selling novels *The Fountainhead* and *Atlas Shrugged*. She developed a philosophical system she called Objectivism.

RASHAD, PHYLICIA – Rashad is an actress, singer, and stage director best known for her role as Clair Huxtable on the NBC sitcom *The Cosby Show*, which ran from 1984 to 1992. She has won many awards, including a Tony Award for best actress in a play (*A Raisin in the Sun-*2004). She was the first black actress to win in that category.

RHIMES, SHONDA – Rhimes is a television producer, screenwriter, and author who is best known for her award-winning television programs *Grey's Anatomy*, *Scandal*, and *How to Get Away with Murder*. In 2007 she was named as one of *Time* magazine's The 100 People Who Help Shape the World.

RICH, ADRIENNE – Rich was an essayist, poet, and radical feminist. She was one of the most widely read poet influencers of the twentieth century and brought women's issues to the forefront of her work.

RICE, CONDOLEEZZA DR. – Dr. Rice is a political scientist and diplomat who served as the secretary of state under the administration of George W. Bush. She was the first African-American female to hold that position. She also acted as President Bush's national security advisor during his first term.

RIETZSCH, LINDSEY – Rietzsch is an author of numerous books, including the acclaimed book *How to Date Your Spouse*. She is an inspirational songwriter, author, entrepreneur, writer, and avid blogger.

RINGELMANN, DANAE – Ringelmann is founder and chief development officer at Indiegogo.

ROBINS, RACHEL – Robins is a writer and businesswoman. She is the creator behind FeelFabToday products. Her passion is exploring and sharing positivity and self-improvement.

ROBINSON, HOLLY – Robinson is a novelist, journalist, and ghostwriter who focuses on pop culture, parenting health, science, and psychology. She has appeared in dozens of national publications.

RODDICK, ANITA – Roddick is a businesswoman, environmental campaigner, and human rights activist best known as the founder of The Body Shop. Her brand was one of the first to prohibit the use of ingredients tested on animals and to promote fair trade with third-world countries.

RODGERS, CRISTEN – Rodgers is a spiritual essayist, author, and blogger. She is the author of three books, all of which focus on the journey into deeper spiritual understanding.

ROMAN, SANAYA – Roman is a writer and audiobook leader who is heavily influenced by the spiritual teachings of Orin. She has authored six books and has numerous weekly and daily affirmations, programs, meditations, and music available.

ROOPLEEN, DR. – Dr. Roopleen is a speaker, motivational counselor, eye surgeon, and author. She has written numerous books to inspire and encourage readers to live life to the fullest.

ROOSEVELT, ELEANOR – Roosevelt was the First Lady of the United States (1933-1945). She was also a politician, diplomat, and activist. She was outspoken and held sometimes unpopular views on expanding the roles for women in the workplace, the civil rights of African and Asian Americans, and the rights of WWII refugees.

ROSENFELD, IRENE BLECKER – Rosenfeld is the chairwoman and CEO of Mondelez International. She has been in the food and beverage industry for over thirty years. She has been named as one of *Forbes*'s The 100 Most Powerful Women numerous times in her career.

ROSS, DIANA – Ross is a singer, songwriter, and record producer. She is most famous for her role as founder and lead member of The Supremes. She was featured in *The Wiz* and was nominated for a Golden Globe and an Academy Award for her role in *Lady Sings the Blues.*

ROTTENBERG, LINDA – Rottenberg is a bestselling author and the CEO and co-founder of Endeavor. She was named one of "America's Best Leaders" by *US News* and is a frequent lecturer at Fortune 500 companies.

ROTH, VERONICA – Roth is a novelist and short-story writer best known for her *New York Times* best-selling *Divergent* trilogy. Her books have won numerous awards and have been made into a blockbuster movie series.

ROWE, NIKKI – Rowe is an author and artist, and *Once a Girl, Now a Woman* is her first book. She resides in Australia.

ROWLING, J.K. – Rowling is a British film producer, screenwriter, and novelist best known for her *Harry Potter* fantasy series. Her *Harry Potter* books are the best-selling book series in history having sold over 400 million copies.

RUDOLPH, WILMA – Rudolph was an American track and field sprinter acclaimed as the fastest woman in the world. She competed in the 1956 and 1960 Olympic Games. She was the first woman to win three gold medals in track during a single Olympic Games.

SALTER-MCNEIL, BRENDA DR. – Dr. Salter-McNeil is a dynamic speaker and author in the ministry of racial, ethnic, and gender reconciliation. She is an associate professor of reconciliation studies in the School of Theology at Seattle Pacific University, where she directs the reconciliation studies program.

SAND, GEORGE – Sand (Amantine-Lucile-Aurore Dupin) was a French novelist and memoirist. She has numerous published works, including short stories, novels, essays, and theatrical works. Sand was well known for her socialist and feminist views.

SANDBERG, SHERYL – Sandberg is the COO of Facebook, founder of the Lean In Foundation and a technology executive, activist, and author. Prior to her position at Facebook, she served as the vice president of global online sales and operations at Google and launched one of its philanthropic programs.

SARANDON, SUSAN – Sarandon is an Academy-Award winning actress. She was appointed a UNICEF Goodwill Ambassador in 1999. Her first film was *Joe*, released in 1970.

SATIR, VIRGINIA – Satir was an author, social worker, and family therapist. She created the Virginia Satir Change Process Model. Satir is regarded as the "Mother of Family Therapy" and has authored numerous well-known books.

SAYERS, DOROTHY – Sayers was a renowned English crime writer, playwright, poet, essayist, translator, and Christian humanist best known for her mystery writing.

SCOTT, JILL – Scott is a poet, actress, model, singer, and songwriter. Her first album went platinum and her two follow-ups went gold. She has appeared in numerous movies and television programs. She is also an advocate for young people and has established a nonprofit organization.

SHALALA, DONNA – Donna Shalala served as United States Secretary of Health and Human Services during the Clinton administration from 1993 to 2001. She is currently president of the Clinton Foundation.

SIMMONS, ANNETTE – Simmons is the founder of Group Process Consulting, which specializes in helping organizations increase their productivity. She is a speaker, community activist, and the author of four books.

SINGER, JUNE – Singer was an analytical psychologist who co-founded the Analytical Psychology Club of Chicago (now the Jung Institute of Chicago) to popularize Carl Jung's theories in the U.S. She is the author of several well-received books.

SINGH, LILLY – Singh is a Canadian YouTube personality, comedian, and actress. She is considered one of the world's highest paid YouTube stars.

SIRLEAF, ELLEN JOHNSON – Sirleaf is the twenty-fourth and current president of Liberia. She is the first elected female head of state in Africa. She was awarded the Nobel Peace Prize in 2011. She is listed as the eighty-third Most Powerful Woman in the World by *Forbes* magazine.

SKLAR, RACHEL – Sklar founded Change the Ratio. She is a Canadian lawyer and a contributor to CNN.

SMITH, B. – Smith (Barbara Elaine) is a model, author, restaurateur, and television host. She was the second black model to appear on the cover of *Mademoiselle* in 1976. She has authored three books and has appeared on numerous television programs.

SORENSON, TONI – Sorenson is an author and an avid blogger. She writes encouraging pieces, dealing with day-to-day issues that plague many—such as anxiety, growth, and personal development.

SOTOMAYOR, SONIA – Sotomayor has been an associate justice of the U.S. Supreme Court since 2009. She is the first judge of Hispanic heritage and the first Latina. She advocates for reform on criminal justice and increased rights for defendants. She has passionate views on issues of race, gender, and ethnic identity.

STEINEM, GLORIA – Steinem is a journalist and social and political activist who was recognized as a leader and spokeswoman for the feminist movement of the late 1960s and 70s. One of her most famous works, *After Black Power, Women's Liberation* (1969), brought her much popularity. She is co-founder of the Women's Media Center.

STRINGER, CHARLAINE VIVIAN – Stringer is the head coach of the Rutgers University women's basketball team. She has amassed one of the most winning records in women's college basketball.

SUMMIT, PAT – Summit was an award-winning basketball coach for the University of Tennessee Lady Volunteers. She amassed 1098 victories, the most in NCAA history.

SWEENEY, ANNE – Sweeney is an American businesswoman and media executive. She formerly held executive roles in Disney Media, Disney-ABC Televisions Group and the Disney Channel.

TAYLOR, SUSAN L. – Taylor is an editor, writer, and journalist who served as editor-in-chief of ESSENCE magazine from 1981 to 2000. She is considered one of the most influential black women in journalism.

TETZLAFF, SUE – Tetzlaff is the co-founder of Capstone Leadership Solutions. She has worked in the healthcare leadership industry for over two decades. She is a board certified nurse and holds advanced degrees in healthcare administration.

THATCHER, MARGARET – Thatcher was a British stateswoman and prime minister of the United Kingdom from 1979 to 1990. She was dubbed "The Iron Lady" because of her uncompromising politics and leadership style.

TOTH, K.L. – Toth is the author of the book *A Test of Faith*.

UCHITEL, APRIL – Uchitel is the chief brand officer of the fashion-tech startup Spring. She has over twenty-five years of experience and spent nine years developing the Dian VonFurstenburg design line.

VANDERBILT, GLORIA – Vanderbilt is an artist, author, actress, fashion designer, heiress, and socialite. She is associated with a successful line of clothing, perfume, and household goods. She is most notably known as an early developer of designer jeans.

VON FURSTENBERG, DIANE – Von Furstenberg is a fashion designer best known for her iconic wrap dress. DVF is a luxury lifestyle brand available in over seventy countries. She is the president of the Council of Fashion Designers of America and has been listed as a powerful woman by *Time* and *Forbes* magazines.

WALKER, ALICE MALSENIOR – Walker is a novelist, short-story writer, poet, and activist. She is well known for her Pulitzer-Prize winning novel *The Color Purple*. Walker coined the term "Womanism," which was created to unite feminists of color under one term.

WEEMS, RENITA J. DR. – Dr. Weems is an ordained minister, biblical scholar, writer, and academic administrator. She has authored several books on women's spirituality and wholeness. She is co-pastor of Ray of Hope Community Church and vice president and academic dean at American Baptist College.

WEI, TIAN – Wei is a leading television anchorwoman in China's international broadcasting industry. She is the host of *World Insight*, a weekly world news and global debate program. She has interviewed world leaders and influential figures from all walks of life.

WEIN, ELIZABETH – Wein is an author and an avid pilot. She has written several books. She focuses on young adult, fantasy, and fiction.

WHARTON, EDITH – Wharton was a Pulitzer Prize-winning American novelist, short-story writer, and designer. She was nominated for the Nobel Prize in Literature in 1927, 1928, and 1930.

WHEATLEY, MARGARET J. – Wheatley is a writer and management consultant who studies organizational behavior through systems thinking, change theory, chaos theory, learning organization, and leadership. She has published six books focused on leadership, organization, and change.

WHITE, KATE – White is editor-in-chief of *Redbook* and *Cosmopolitan* and is an author, coach, and speaker. Her books have appeared on *The New York Times* best-sellers list.

WHITMAN, MEG – Whitman is the president and CEO of Hewlett Packard Enterprises, the former CEO of eBay, and a former Republican candidate for California Governor.

WILDEROTTER, MAGGIE – Wilderotter was CEO of Frontier Communications (2004-2015) and executive chairman of the same company until 2016. Under her direction, the company grew from a $1 billion phone company to a $10 billion voice and video provider.

WILLIAMSON, MARIANNE – Williamson is a spiritual teacher, author, and lecturer who has published eleven books, four of which were *New York Times* best-sellers. She is the founder of Project Angel Food and the co-founder of The Peace Alliance.

WILLS, HEIDI – Wills served as a Seattle, Washington, council member in the early 2000s. She found it important for the civil rights and liberties of all citizens to be upheld, including those of immigrated citizens.

WINFREY, OPRAH – Winfrey is a media proprietor, talk show host, actress, producer, and philanthropist. She is best known for her talk show, *The Oprah Winfrey Show*, and now has her own television network. She was awarded the Presidential Medal of Freedom in 2013.

WINTOUR, ANNE (DAME) – Wintour is editor in chief of *Vogue*, a position she has held since 1988. In addition, she is the artistic director for Conde Nast, *Vogue*'s publisher.

WOLLSTONECRAFT, MARY – Wollstonecraft was an English writer, philosopher, and advocate of women's rights. Her most famous work, *A Vindication of the Rights of Women* (1972), argues that men and women should be treated equitably. She is considered one of the founding feminist philosophers.

WU, NORA – Wu is the vice chairwoman of PwC Global. She speaks at a vast range of business conventions, seminars, and events, spanning a wide array of business and leadership-related topics.

YAMANOUCHI, MIYA – Yamanouchi is an Austrailian-based empowerment counselor who specializes in sexual health. She works with both men and women.

YOUSAFZAI, MALALA – Yousafzai is a Pakastani activist for the importance of education for women and girls and is the youngest-ever Nobel Prize Laureate. In 2012, a gunman attempted to assassinate her for her outspokenness about education for all. She has since campaigned internationally for education rights for women worldwide.

YOVANOFF, BRENNA – Yovanoff is the author of over seven books. She is a young adult, science fiction, and fantasy author. Yovanoff is also an avid blogger with a unique Internet presence.

ZHU, PEARL – Zhu has worked in the IT, e-commerce, and international trading communities for over twenty-one years. She is the author of numerous books and advocates for business innovation and cultural evolution.

—◊—

Biographical information was obtained from various Internet-based sources, including but not limited to author websites and Biography.com. While the TransPorter Group strived to make the information in each bio as timely and accurate as possible, TransPorter makes no claims, promises, or guarantees about the accuracy, completeness, or adequacy of the contents of these bios, and expressly disclaims liability for errors and omissions in the contents of this compilation.

Defining Leadership

1. King, Coretta Scott. 2017. *My Life, My Love, My Legacy.* New York: Henry Holt and Co., Kindle edition, loc 984.

2. Rosabeth Moss Kanter in Graham, Pauline (ed). 2003. *Mary Parker Follet: Prophet of Management, A Celebration of Writings from the 1920s.* Washington, D.C.: Beard Books, p. xiv.

3. Retrieved November 21, 2016, from https://www.brainyquote.com/quotes/quotes/r/rosalynnca126340.html

4. Adrian, Lorne (compiled by). 1997. *The Most Important Thing I Know: Life Lessons from Colin Powell, Stephen Covey, Maya Angelou and Over 75 Other Eminent Individuals.* New York: Cader Books.

5. St. John, Bonnie and Darcy Deane. 2012. *How Great Women Lead: A Mother-Daughter Adventure into the Lives of Women Shaping the World.* New York: Hachette Book Group, p. 53.

6. Summit, Pat with Sally Jenkins. 2013. *Sum It Up: A Thousand and Ninety-Eight Victories, A Couple of Irrelevant Losses and a Life in Perspective.* New York: Crown Archetype, p. 219.

7. St. John, Bonnie and Darcy Deane. 2012. *How Great Women Lead: A Mother-Daughter Adventure into the Lives of Women Shaping the World.* New York: Hachette Book Group, p. 53.

8. Modhiya, Divya M., "Women Empowerment in India: A Burning Issue." *International Journal of Social Impact*, Volume 1, Issue 2, April-June 2016

9. Takeuchi, Lisa Cullen. "The Rules According to Dee Dee Myers," Time.com, February 28, 2009, http://content.time.com/time/arts/article/0,8599,1718519-2,00.html

10. Subdrink, Laurie. 2015. *Leading with GRIT: Inspiring Action and Accountability with Generosity.* Hoboken: John Wiley & Sons.

11. Porter, Jeanne. 2000. *Leading Ladies: Transformative Biblical Images for Women's Leadership.* Philadelphia: InnisFree Press, p. 26.

12. Summit, Pat with Sally Jenkins. 2013. *Sum It Up: A Thousand and Ninety-Eight Victories, A Couple of Irrelevant Losses and a Life in Perspective.* New York: Crown Archetype, p. 240.

13. Queen Elizabeth II addresses the United Nations General Assembly July 6, 2010, 64 General Assembly, New York at UN Headquarters.

14. Jameson, Jill. 2012. *Leadership in Post-Compulsory Education: Inspiring Leaders of the Future.* New York: Routledge.

15. Scott, Mark. "Himanshu Bhatia stays alert for opportunity at Rose International." *Smart Business.* June 1, 2011, http://www.sbnonline.com/article/himanshu-bhatia-stays-alert-for-opportunity-at-rose-international/

16. Hauss, Charles. 1996. *Beyond Confrontation: Transforming the New World Order.* Connecticut: Praeger Publishers.

17. Amukobole, Micah. 2012. *Character-Centered Leadership: Principles and Practice of Effective Leading.* Nairobi: Evangel Publishing House.

18. https://www.brainyquote.com/quotes/authors/i/irene_rosenfeld.html

19. Steinbrecher, Susan. "50 Shades of Red: Quotes That Will Inspire You to Lead From the Heart." Inc.com, http://www.inc.com/susan-steinbrecher/50-shades-of-red-50-quotes-that-will-inspire-you-to-lead-from-the-heart.html

20. "10 Women in Leadership Share Their Secrets to Success." FastCompany.com, June 17, 2014.

21. McKenzie, Vashti M. 1996, 2011. *Not Without a Struggle, Leadership Development for African American Women in Ministry.* Cleveland: Pilgrim Press.

22. Marsha Clark, Leadership Consultant and Executive Coach, e-mail correspondence,

December 14, 2016

23. Barton, Ruth Haley. 2008. *Strengthening the Soul of Your Leadership: Seeking God in the Crucible of Ministry.* Downers Grove: InterVarsity Press p, 217.

24. "10 Women in Leadership Share Their Secrets to Success." FastCompany.com, June 17, 2014.

25. Porter, Jeanne. 2000. *Leading Ladies: Transformative Biblical Images for Women's Leadership.* Philadelphia: Innisfree Press, Kindle edition, p. 13.

26. St. John, Bonnie and Darcy Deane. 2012. *How Great Women Lead: A Mother-Daughter Adventure Into the Lives of Women Shaping the World.* New York: Center Street (Hachette Book Group), p. 15.

27. Stringer, Vivian C. with Laura Tucker. 2008. *Standing Tall, A Memoir of Tragedy and Triumph.* New York: Crown Archetype.

28. Summit, Pat with Sally Jenkins. 2013. *Sum It Up: A Thousand and Ninety-Eight Victories, A Couple of Irrelevant Losses and a Life in Perspective.* New York: Crown Archetype, p. 240.

29. "10 Women in Leadership Share Their Secrets to Success." FastCompany.com, June 17, 2014.

30. Summit, Pat with Sally Jenkins. 2013. *Sum It Up: A Thousand and Ninety-Eight Victories, A Couple of Irrelevant Losses and a Life in Perspective.* New York: Crown Archetype, p. 240.

31. King, Coretta Scott. 2017. *My Life, My Love, My Legacy.* New York: Henry Holt and Co., loc 390, Kindle edition.

32. Bridges, Frances. "What Madeline Albright Wants Women to Know." *Forbes*, June 24, 2015, http://www.forbes.com/sites/francesbridges/2015/06/24/what-madeline-albright-wants-women-to-know/#3556cc1e64a7

33. *Profiles in Diversity Journal.* http://www.diversityjournal.com/15214-deborah-gillis-catalyst/

34. ibid

35. Hewlett, Sylvia Ann. 2014. *Executive Presence: The Missing Link Between Merit and Success.* New York: Harper Collins ebooks, p. 24.

36. Krawcheck, Sallie. 2017. *Own It: The Power of Women at Work.* New York: Crown Business, Kindle Books, loc 1310.

37. Jones-Deweever, Ph.D., Avis A. 2016. *How Exceptional Black Women Lead: Unlocking the Secrets to Phenomenal Success in Career and Life.* Woodbridge: Incite Publishing Company, p. 85.

38. ibid.

39. St. John, Bonnie and Darcy Deane. 2012. *How Great Women Lead: A Mother-Daughter Adventure Into the Lives of Women Shaping the World.* New York: Center Street (Hachette Book Group), p. 33.

40. ibid, p. 294.

41. Rampton, Kristy. "50 Motivational Quotes from Disruptive, Trailblazing, Inspiring Women Leaders." Entrepreneur.com, May 11, 2015, https://www.entrepreneur.com/article/245810

42. http://indianexpress.com/photos/lifestyle-gallery/lakme-fashion-week-2017-avantika-malik-and-mallika-dua-walk-the-ramp-for-designer-shahni-himanshu-4502876/2/

43. https://www.entrepreneur.com/article/245810

44. "10 Women in Leadership Share Their Secrets to Success." FastCompany.com, June 17, 2014

45. ibid

46. Lucas, Suzanne. "Bossiness Is Not a Leadership Trait." Inc.com, February 13, 2014,

http://www.inc.com/suzanne-lucas/bossiness-is-not-a-leadership-trait-no-matter-what-sheryl-sandberg-says.html

47. Harris, Carla A. 2009. *Expect to Win: 10 Proven Strategies for Thriving in the Workplace*. New York: Hudson Street Press, p. 84.

48. Hesselbein, Frances. 2007. *Hesselbein on Leadership (J-B Leader To Leader Institute)*. San Francisco: Jossey-Bass, Kindle edition, loc 481.

49. Ibid

Influential Leadership

50. http://www.afr.com/news/meet-australias-100-women-of-influence-20121011-jiosz

51. Leaders and Revolutionaries: Oprah Winfrey, Condoleezza Rice, *Time*. May 8, 2006.

52. Farrel, Pam. 2006. *Woman of Influence: Ten Traits of Those Who Want to Make a Difference*. Downers Grove: InterVarsity Press.

53. Dearman, Nancy. "Why We Need More (Women) Leaders," *Harvard Business Review*. September 5, 2013, https://hbr.org/2013/09/why-we-need-more-women-leaders

54. Lillie, Ben. "In debates, watch for signs of warmth: Q&A with Amy Cuddy." TedBlog, October 1, 2012, http://blog.ted.com/in-debates-watch-for-signs-of-warmth-qa-with-amy-cuddy/

55. Ransby, Barbara. 2003. *Ella Baker and the Black Freedom Movement*. Univ. of North Carolina Press.

56. Sims, Bennett J. 1997. *Servanthood: Leadership for the Third Millennium*. Cambridge: Cowley Publications. (Also argued to be an African proverb of unknown specific origin.)

57. https://www.goodreads.com/author/quotes/1078349.Wilma_Rudolph

58. Michelle Obama at The Young African Women Leaders Forum, Soweto, South Africa, Regina Mundi Church, June 22, 2011.

59. Lear, L. 2008. *Beatrix Potter: The Extraordinary Life of a Victorian Genius*. New York: St. Martin's Press (Penguin UK).

60. Goodrich, Richelle. 2015. *Making Wishes: Quotes, Thoughts & a Little Poetry for Every Day of the Year*. Createspace.

61. Buchanan, Ph.D., Laurie. "Sphere of Influence," *Tuesdays with Laurie* (Blog), August 26, 2014.

62. Malala Yousafzai in her Peter J Gomes Humanitarian of the Year Acceptance Speech at Harvard University, September 2013.

63. O'Donnell, Paul. "Victoria Osteen Says, 'Love Your Life.'" http://www.beliefnet.com/columnists/idolchatter/2008/11/victoria-osteen-says-love-your.html

64. Gibbs, Nancy. "The Ties that Bind 100," Time.com, April 24, 2014.

65. http://www.azquotes.com/quote/865531

66. Reingold, Jennifer. "PepsiCo's CEO Was Right, Now What?," June 5, 2015, Fortune.com

67. Edwards, Tryon. 1927, 2011. *The New Dictionary of Thoughts: A Cyclopedia of Quotations from the Best Authors of the World, both Ancient and Modern*. Hoar Press.

68. http://blog.cleveland.com/metro/2009/08/cleveland_state_university_adm.html

69. Steinbecher, Susan. "50 Shades of Red: Quotes That Will Inspire You to Lead from the Heart." Inc.com, http://www.inc.com/susan-steinbrecher/50-shades-of-red-50-quotes-that-will-inspire-you-to-lead-from-the-heart.html

70. Frank, Anne. 1993. *Anne Frank: Diary of a Young Girl*. New York: Bantam Books (original copyright, 1952 by Otto H. Frank).

71. Dr. Renita Weems, Twitter @somethingwithin October 24, 2016

72. https://www.goodreads.com/author/quotes/95614.Whoopi_Goldberg

73. http://www.goodreads.com/quotes/5934-i-ve-learned-that-people-will-forget-what-you-said-people

74. Wharton, Edith. 1920. *The Age of Innocence*. London: D. Appleton and Company.

75. Hutyra, Hannah. "107 Audrey Hepburn Quotes That Will Inspire You." Keepinspiringme.com

76. Steinbrecher, Susan. "50 Quotes That Will Inspire You to Lead from the Heart." HuffingtonPost, 3/19/2015, http://www.huffingtonpost.com/susan-steinbrecher/50-quotes-that-will-inspi_b_6897644.html

77. Michelle Obama at the Democratic National Convention September 4, 2012, in Charlotte, N.C.

78. Malala Yousafzai, July 12, 2013, UN General Assembly Address, United Nations, New York

79. https://www.brainyquote.com/quotes/authors/r/rosa_parks.html

80. 2008 Women's Conference at Brigham Young University in Provo, UT.

81. http://womenforone.com/portfolio/ive-always-believed-that-one-womans-success-can-only-help-another-womans-success-gloria-vanderbilt/

82. Feser, Claudio. 2016. *When Execution Isn't Enough: Decoding Inspirational Leadership*. Hoboken: Wiley Publishers.

83. Riley, Lesley. 2014. *Inspirational Quotes Illustrated: Art and Words to Motivate*. Ohio: Northlight Books.

84. Kipperman, Sue. 2008. *Bootstraps: A Woman's Guide to Personal Power in a Victim-Driven World*. New York: iUniverse Inc.

85. http://theslayathomemom.com/2016/02/01/one-year-later/

86. Petersen, Randy and Robin Shreeves. 2014. *The One Year Women in Christian History Devotional: Daily Inspiration from God's Work in the Lives of Women*. Carol Stream: Tydale House.

87. Montgomery, Lucy Maud. 1908. *Anne of Green Gables*. Boston: LC Page and Co.

88. As reported by Ralph Waldo Emerson in *Memoirs of Margaret Fuller Ossoli* (1884) Vol. 1, Pt. 4.

89. Angelou, Maya. "Be a Rainbow in Someone Else's Cloud," HuffPost OWN, Oprah's Master Class, January 16, 2011

90. Williamson, Marianne. 1992. A *Return to Love: Reflections on the Principles of "A Course in Miracles."* New York: Harper One.

91. Denenberg, Dennis and Lorraine Roscoe. 1947, 2016. *50 American Heroes Every Kid Should Meet*. Brookfield: The Millbrook Press.

92. Marcus, Bonnie. 2015. *The Politics of Promotion: How High-Achieving Women Get Ahead and Stay Ahead*. Hoboken: John Wiley & Sons, Inc.

93. Chung, Grace. "Buffett, Sara Blakely, and Other Billionaires." Forbes.com, May 9, 2016, http://www.forbes.com/sites/gracechung/2016/03/09/20-favorite-quotes-from-warren-buffett-sara-blakely-and-other-billionaires/#389c91951f0d

94. Schwantes, Marcel. "101 Inspiring Quotes From Trailblazing Women in Honor of Today's Holiday." Inc.com, September 22, 2016.

95. Hale, Cynthia. 2010. *I'm a Piece of Work! Sisters Shaped by God*. Valley Forge: Judson Press, p. 12.

Authentic Leadership

96. "10 Women in Leadership Share Their Secrets to Success." FastCompany.com, June 17, 2014.

97. https://www.brainyquote.com/quotes/authors/e/eleanor_roosevelt.html

98. Collins, Patricia Hill. 1990. *Black Feminist Thought: Knowledge, Consciousness, and the Politics of Empowerment, Perspectives on Gender.* Vol. 2. New York: Routledge, p. 34.

99. King, Coretta Scott. 2017. *My Life, My Love, My Legacy.* New York: Henry Holt and Co., Kindle edition, loc 1206.

100. Interview for Press Association (10th Anniversary as Prime Minister), May 3, 1989, with Chris Moncrieff, Thatcher Archive, UK

101. Naylor, Gloria. 1988. *Mama Day.* New York: Random House, p. 114.

102. "Aspire to Lead: Why Confidence is Necessary for Women's Leadership," AIESEC, March 24, 2015, http://aiesec.org/aspire-to-lead-confidence-in-women-leadership/

103. Kanter, Rosabeth Moss. 2004. *Confidence: How Winning and Losing Streaks Begin and End.* New York: Crown Business.

104. Weems, Renita. 2002. *Showing Mary: How Women Can Share Prayers, Wisdom, and the Blessings of God.* New York: Walk Worthy Press, loc 766, Kindle edition.

105. "10 Women in Leadership Share Their Secrets to Success." FastCompany.com, June 17, 2014.

106. Robins, Rachel. 2013. *How to Feel Good About Yourself—Boost Your Confidence & Tackle Low Self-Esteem. Packed with Self-Improvement Techniques, Positive Thinking Tips & Inspirational Quotes.* Dreamstime

107. Toni Sorenson. 2016. *The Great Brain Cleanse Quotes.* Goodreads.com.

108. Kanter, Rosabeth Moss. 2004. *Confidence: How Winning and Losing Streaks Begin and End.* New York: Crown Business.

109. Fisher, Lauren Alexis. "30 Empowering Quotes from Women Who Dare." *Harper's Bazaar.* May 30, 2016, http://www.harpersbazaar.com/culture/features/a4056/empowering-female-quotes/

110. U.S. Senate, The Equal Rights Amendment: Hearings before the Subcommittee on Constitutional Amendments of the Senate Committee on the Judiciary, 91st Congress, 2nd Session, 5-7 May, 1970, p. 331-335, https://www.wwnorton.com/college/history/archive/reader/trial/directory/1959_1970/10_ch35_02.htm

111. http://www.mountunion.edu/dr-charleyse-pratt-presents-keynote-address

112. Sandburg, Sheryl and Nell Scovell. 2013. *Lean In: Women, Work, and the Will to Lead.* New York: Knopf.

113. Hillary Hangout 06.01.2016, Daily Kos, as quoted from an Interview with Katie Couric, Super Tuesday, Chappaqua, N.Y, February 6, 2008

114. St. John, Bonnie and Darcy Deane. 2012. *How Great Women Lead: A Mother-Daughter Adventure into the Lives of Women Shaping the World.* New York: Hachette Book Group, p. 54.

115. ibid, p. 53.

116. Roosevelt, Eleanor. 1960. *You Learn by Living.* New York: Harper and Row Inc.

117. Schnall, Marianne Schnall. "Madeleine Albright: An Exclusive Interview." *The Huffington Post,* 6/15/2010/ http://www.huffingtonpost.com/marianne-schnall/madeleine-albright-an-exc_b_604418.html

118. Halima Aden, Miss Minnesota USA pageant contestant.

119. Interview by Andrew Goldberg, "How Diane von Furstenberg is Like a Cowboy," *The*

New York Times Magazine, June 28, 2013.

120. Schmitz, Melanie. "5 Hillary Clinton Quotes About Struggle that Will Make You Feel Better about Your Life." June 16, 2016, https://www.bustle.com/articles/90515-5-hillary-clinton-quotes-about-struggle-that-will-make-you-feel-better-about-your-life

121. Interview with Lynn Sherr ABC Correspondent, preceding the Ruth Bader Ginsberg Distinguished Lecture on Women and the Law delivered by Katherine Sullivan at Stanford University Law School. Read in "Justice Ginsberg Recalls Bias, Expresses Concerns" by Kristen Choo, Womensnews.org, Nov. 20, 2000.

122. ICICI's Chandra Kochhar: "Whenever there's a Challenge, I see an Opportunity," February 6, 2008, Interview with Michael Useem at the World Economic Forum at Davos

123. Walker, Alice. 1983. *In Search of Our Mothers' Gardens: Womanist Prose*. New York: Harcourt Inc.

124. Husted, Wes. 2014. *The Seven Things You Should Know About Being a Leader*. Indiegopublishing.com: IndieGo Publishing LLC

125. Hurley, Kathleen and Priscilla Schumway (Eds.). 2015. *Real Women, Real Leaders: Surviving and Succeeding in the Business World*. Hoboken: John Wiley & Sons Inc.

126. Schor, Rebecca Einstein (Ed.) and Alysa Mendelson Graf. 2016. *The Sacred Calling: Four Decades of Women in the Rabbinate*. New York: CCAR Press

127. Marcus, Bonnie. 2015. *The Politics of Promotion: How High-Achieving Women Get Ahead and Stay Ahead*. Hoboken: John Wiley & Sons, Inc.

128. "Her Sassiest Quotes of All Time." *Marie Claire*, December 10, 2015, http://www.marieclaire.co.uk/uncategorised/j-lo-her-sassiest-quotes-of-all-time-61328

129. Haden, Jeff. "50 Inspiring Motivational Quotes to Increase Your Confidence." Inc.com, http://www.inc.com/jeff-haden/50-inspiring-motivational-quotes-to-increase-your-confidence.html

130. Malone, Noreen. "Can Women Have it All? Beyonce Says Yes." *New Republic*, January 26, 2013, https://newrepublic.com/article/112214/beyonces-message-women-can-have-it-all

131. Akdeniz, Can. 2015. *7 Habits of Highly Self-Confident People*. Kindle e-book

132. 5 Amazing Quotes from Actress and Entrepreneur Blake Lively, Makers.com, September 22, 2015, http://www.makers.com/blog/best-blake-lively-quotes

133. Curie, Eve. 1937, 2001. *Madame Curie: A Biography*. Second edition, New York: Da Capo Press, p. 116.

134. https://www.brainyquote.com/quotes/authors/l/lilly_singh.html

135. DarConte, Ed., Lorrine. 2001. *Pride Matters: Quotes to Inspire Your Personal Best*. Kansas City: Andrews McMeel Publishing.

136. Haden, Jeff. "50 Inspiring Motivational Quotes to Increase Your Confidence." Inc.com, http://www.inc.com/jeff-haden/50-inspiring-motivational-quotes-to-increase-your-confidence.html

137. Barton, Ruth Haley. 2008. *Strengthening the Soul of Your Leadership*. Downers Grove: InterVasrity Press, p. 217.

138. http://www.quotesigma.com/45-famous-quotes-helen-keller/

139. Hewlett, Sylvia Ann. 2014. *Executive Presence: The Missing Link Between Merit and Success*. New York: Harper Collins e-books, p. 10.

140. ibid, p. 6

141. Hesselbein, Frances. 2007. *Hesselbein on Leadership (J-B Leader To Leader Institute)*. New York: Jossey-Bass, Kindle edition, loc 118.

142. Jones-Deweever, Ph.D., Avis A. 2016. *How Exceptional Black Women Lead: Unlocking the*

Secrets to Phenomenal Success in Career and Life. Woodbridge: Incite Publishing Company, p. 50.

143. Lindsey, Connie. "Life Lessons from the C-Suite: Connie Lindsey." http://www.socialifechicago.com/2016/10/24/life-lessons-from-the-c-suite-connie-lindsey/

144. Harris. Carla A. 2009. *Expect to Win: 10 Proven Strategies for Thriving in the Workplace.* New York: Hudson Press, p. 4.

Courageous Leadership

145. Ettus, Samantha. "Inspiring Quotes from 100 Extraordinary Women." *The Huffington Post,* January 23, 2015.

146. "10 Women in Leadership Share Their Secrets to Success." *FastCompany.* June 17, 2014.

147. Dew, Sheri. "This Is a Test, This Is Only a Test," from a talk given May 1, 1998 at Brigham Young University-Women's Conference.

148. Oliver, Vanessa. 2013 *Healing Home: Health and Homelessness in the Life Stories of Young Women.* Toronto: University of Toronto Press.

149. Dew, Sheri. 2001. "Knowing Who You Are—and Who You Have Always Been," https://womensconference.byu.edu/sites/womensconference.ce.byu.edu/files/dew_sheri_2.pdf

150. Keyes, Allison. "Johnnetta B. Cole Is a Force of Nature." *The Root.* October 19, 2016, http://www.theroot.com/johnnetta-b-cole-is-a-force-of-nature-1790857328

151. Jones-Deweever, Ph.D., Avis A. 2016. *How Exceptional Black Women Lead: Unlocking the Secrets to Phenomenal Success in Career and Life.* Woodbridge: Incite Publishing Company, p. 28.

152. Roosevelt, Eleanor. 1960. *You Learn by Living.* New York: Harper and Row Inc.

153. St. John, Bonnie and Darcy Deane. 2012. *How Great Women Lead: A Mother-Daughter Adventure into the Lives of Women Shaping the World.* New York: Hachette Book Group, p. 17.

154. Winfrey, Oprah. "What Oprah Knows for Sure About Always Saying Yes." Oprah.com, August 15, 2000.

155. Kravetz, Stacy. 1999. *Girl Boss: Running the Show Like the Big Chicks.* Girl Press (introduction by Gillian Anderson).

156. Williams, Terrie M. 2008. *Black Pain: It Just Looks Like We're Not Hurting.* New York: Scribner.

157. Owajoba, Tolulope. "Inspiring Quotes from 100 Extraordinary Women." WAAW Foundation, January 28, 2015, http://waawfoundation.org/2015/01/28/inspiring-quotes-from-100-extraordinary-women/

158. Ward, Marguerite. "PepsiCo CEO shares her 3-step path for advancing your career," December 28, 2016, http://www.cnbc.com/2016/12/28/pepsico-ceo-shares-her-3-step-path-to-advancing-your-career.html

159. "Claiming an Education," Adrienne Rich's convocation speech at Douglass College, 1977.

160. Rosenberg, Eli. "'To Age Is a Sin': In Blunt Speech, Madonna Confronts Bias in Various Forms." *The New York Times,* December 10, 2016.

161. Parks, Rosa with Gregory J. Reed. 1994, 2000. *Quiet Strength.* Grand Rapids: Zondervan.

162. February 24, 2016, https://www.exceptionalchicagoans.com/connie-lindsey

Power-Full Leadership

163. Graham, Pauline (Ed). 1995. *Mary Parker Follett Prophet of Management.* Washington, D.C.: Beard Books, p. 101.

164. ibid, p. 103

165. Rowling, J.K. 2015. *Very Good Lives: The Fringe Benefits of Failure and the Importance of Imagination.* New York: Little Brown and Company (based on a 2008 commencement speech given at Harvard University).

166. Michelle Obama's speech at the Democratic National Convention in Philadelphia, July 25, 2016

167. Bea, Shana and J. Chavae. 2014. *Her Crown: A Journey of Self Love from a Girl to a Queen.* Lulu Press Inc.

168. Collins, Ronald. 2016. *5000+ Quotes for the Seeker of Riches.* Pubished by Ronalds Collins.

169. Roman, Sanaya. 1986, 2011. *Living with Joy: Keys to Personal Power and Spiritual Transformation.* Tiburon: H J Kramer Inc.

170. Burg, Ann E. 2009. *All the Broken Pieces.* New York: Scholastic Press.

171. Nazarian, Vera. 2010. *The Perpetual Calendar of Inspiration: Old Wisdom for a New World,* Highgate Center: Norilana Books.

172. Bonta, Vanna. 1995. *Flight: A Quantum Fiction Novel.* Meridian House

173. Nazarian, Vera. 2010. *The Perpetual Calendar of Inspiration: Old Wisdom for a New World,* Highgate Center: Norilana Books.

174. Akita, Lailah Gifty. 2015. *Pearls of Wisdom: Great Mind.*

175. Schwantes, Marcel. "101 Inspiring Quotes from Trailblazing Women," September 22, 2016, http://www.inc.com/marcel-schwantes/101-inspiring-quotes-from-trailblazing-women-in-honor-of-todays-holiday.html

176. Capretto, Lisa. "Michelle Obama to Young Girls: 'What's in Your Brain Is Really Useful. Do Not Hide it.'" *The Huffington Post,* December 20, 2016, http://www.huffingtonpost.com/entry/michelle-obama-message-to-girls_us_585858fbe4b03904470a5034

177. Schwantes, Marcel. "101 Inspiring Quotes from Trailblazing Women," September 22, 2016., http://www.inc.com/marcel-schwantes/101-inspiring-quotes-from-trailblazing-women-in-honor-of-todays-holiday.html

178. "85 Quotes from Black Women to Inspire You." *For Harriet,* http://forharriet.com/2012/03/85-quotes-from-black-women-to-inspire.html#axzz4S5TIwaKU

179. Young, David. 2012. *Rebound Strong: Hope and Strength or Life's Toughest Challenges.* Round Rock: WindRunner Press.

180. Hale, Cynthia. 2010. *I'm a Piece of Work! Sisters Shaped by God.* Valley Forge: Judson Forge, p. 12

181. http://www.azquotes.com/author/6502-Dorothy_Height

182. Forbes, Moira. "7 Career Lessons from Billionaire Abigail Johnson." *Forbes,* https://www.forbes.com/sites/moiraforbes/2013/11/01/seven-career-lessons-from-billionaire-abigail-johnson/#2ee8783e76a1

183. Blanton, Shannon and Charles Kegley. 2017, 2015, 2014. *World Politics Trend and Transformation 2016-2017 Edition.* Boston: Cengage Learning.

184. "33 Inspirational Quotes all Women Need to Hear." Bright Drops.com, http://brightdrops.com/inspirational-quotes-for-women

185. Ashford, Mary-Wynne and Guy Dauncey. 2006. *Enough Violence: 101 Solutions to Violence, Terror, and Bloodshed.* Gabriola Island: New Society Publishers.

186. Hining, Deborah Griffitts. 2011. *Money Is No Object: How to Get the Life You Dream of Even if You Think You Can't Afford It.* Durham: Light Messages.

187. Lorde, Audre. 1997, 1980. *The Cancer Journals.* San Francisco: Aunt Lute Books.

188. Hengen, Shannon and Ashley Thomson. 2007. *Margaret Atwood: A Reference Guide, 1988-2005.* Lanham: Scarecrow Press.

189. Merryweather, Cheish. "20 Success Secrets from Female Entrepreneurs." October 20, 2015, Thetalko.com, http://www.thetalko.com/20-success-secrets-from-female-entrepreneurs/7/

190. Rice, Franchesca. "Maya Angelou: An Extraordinarily Wise Woman." *Marie Claire*, May 28, 2014, Marie Claire, http://www.marieclaire.co.uk/uncategorised/maya-angelou-an-extraordinarily-wise-woman-84132

191. hooks, bell. 1990. *Yearning: Race, Gender, and Cultural Politics.* Boston: South End Press, p. 102.

192. Rietzsch, Lindsey K. 2014. *The Happy Lady: Making the Best of What Life Gives Us.* Layton: Visintra Group LLC.

193. Hesselbein, Frances. 2007. *Hesselbein on Leadership (J-B Leader To Leader Institute).* New York: Jossey-Bass, Kindle edition, loc 216.

Inclusive Leadership

194. Asmussen, Kirsten. 2011. *The Evidence-based Parenting Practitioner's Handbook.* New York and Canada: Routledge.

195. Vaidyanathan, Rajini. "Before there was Hillary Clinton, there was Shirley Chisholm." *BBC News*, January 26, 2016, http://www.bbc.com/news/magazine-35057641

196. Kassem, Suzy. 2010. *Rise Up and Salute the Sun: The Writings of Suzy Kassem.* Awakenedpress.com: Awakened Press.

197. Mowafi, Amy. 2008. *Fe-mail: The Trials and Tribulations of Being a Good Egyptian Girl.* Enigma Books.

198. Sandburg, Sheryl and Nell Scovell. 2013 *Lean In: Women, Work and the Will to Lead.* New York: Knopf, p. 8.

199. Davis, Shoshana. "Marillyn Hewson, Lockheed Martin's first female CEO, on running the world's largest defense contractor." CBS News, http://www.cbsnews.com/news/marillyn-hewson-lockheed-martins-first-female-ceo-on-running-worlds-largest-defense-contractor/ as quoted from an interview with Norah O'Donnell on *CBS This Morning*.

200. Wollstonecraft, Mary. 2004. *A Vindication of the Rights of Women.* London: Penguin Classics (first published in 1792).

201. Guillain, Charlotte. 2015. *Stories of Women's Suffrage: Votes for Women!.* London: Heinemann.

202. https://www.brainyquote.com/quotes/quotes/m/margepierc100505.html

203. Remarks by First Lady Michelle Obama at the Summit of the Mandela Washington Fellowship for Young African Leaders, Omni Shoreham Hotel, Washington, D.C, July 30, 2015.

204. Obenchain, Kathryn M. and Julie L. Pennington. 2015. *Educating for Critical Democratic Literacy: Integrating Social Studies and Literacy in the Elementary Classroom.* New York: Routledge.

205. Vaidyanathan, Rajini. "Before there was Hillary Clinton, there was Shirley Chisholm." *BBC News*, January 26, 2016, http://www.bbc.com/news/magazine-35057641

206. Lemmon, Gayle Tzemach. "The Hillary Doctrine." *Newsweek*, March 6, 2011, Newsweek.com, http://www.newsweek.com/hillary-doctrine-66105

207 Cleveland, Christena. 2013. *Disunity in Christ: Uncovering the Hidden Forces that Keep Us Apart.* Downers Grove: IVP Books, p. 40.

208. Salter-McNeil, Brenda. 2014. *Roadmap to Reconciliation: Moving Communities Into Unity, Wholeness, and Justice.* Downers Grove: InterVasrity Press, Kindle edition, p. 364, .

209. A quote often attributed to Ayn Rand as "The question isn't who is going to let me. It's who is going to stop me," inspired by dialog in her 1943 novel *The Fountainhead*, http://quoteinvestigator.com/2013/10/11/let-me/

210. Luscombe, Belinda. "Confidence Woman," Time.com, March 7, 2013

211. ibid

212. Congressional Record, V. 149, PT 12, June 20–July7, 2003, edited by U.S. Congress

213. Sullivan, Kathleen. "The State of Truth: Supreme Court Justices Speak," "Constitutionalizing Women's Equality," Winter 2001, *The Record* of the Association of the Bar of the City of New York, 56:1.

214. Huffington, Arianna. 2015. *Thrive: The Third Metric to Redefining Success and Creating a Life of Well-Being, Wisdom and Wonder.* New York: Harmony Books.

215. Martina Navratilova Biography, *A&E Television Networks*, December 18, 2014, biography.com, http://www.biography.com/people/martina-navratilova-9420862

216. Harper, Hill. 2008. *Letters to a Young Sister: DeFINE Your Destiny.* New York: Gotham Books.

217. Barnard College Commencement, May 17, 2011, New York.

218. Redd, Nola Taylor. "Mae Jemison: Astronaut Biography," Space.com, August 17, 2012, http://www.space.com/17169-mae-jemison-biography.html

219. Fisher, Lauren Alexis. "30 Inspiring Quotes From Women who Dare." *Harper's Bazaar,* May 30, 2016

220. Ford, Lynn E. 2008. *Encyclopedia of Women and American Politics (Facts on File Library of American History.* New York, July 4, 1876, Declaration of the Rights of Women.

221. Cleveland, Christena. 2013. *Disunity in Christ: Uncovering the Hidden Forces that Keep Us Apart.* Downers Grove: IVP Books, p. 62.

222. Holly Robinson, "Our Muses, Ourselves: Why Women Like Me Run Away from Home." *The Huffington Post,* February 10, 2011, 1:24 p.m., http://www.huffingtonpost.com/holly-robinson/our-muses-ourselves-why-w_b_821122.html

223. Wei, Tian. "China Can and Must Close its Gender Gap." *The Huffington Post,* November 6, 2016, 2:49 p.m., http://www.huffingtonpost.com/tian-wei/china-can-and-must-close-_b_6116578.html

224. Roth, Veronica. 2013. *Allegiant.* New York: HarperCollins.

225. Glass, Alana. "Condoleezza Rice Talks Diversity and Inclusion in Sports." Forbes.com, February 5, 2016, 2:53 p.m.

226. Interview with Ava DuVernay, director of the film *Selma,* http://aalbc.com/reviews/ava-duvernay-2014.html

227. Mlambo-Ngcuka, Phumzile. "Why we need new allies for gender quality." World Economic Forum, January 18, 2015, https://www.weforum.org/agenda/2015/01/why-we-need-new-allies-for-gender-equality/

228. Corsan, Gerard. 2005. *Heritage, Museums, and Galleries: An Introductory Reader.* New York and Canada: Routledge.

229. Patti Digh. 2008. *Life Is a Verb: 37 Days to Wake Up, Be Mindful, and Live Intentionally!* Guilford: skirt!

230. "Marilyn Hewson: Building an Inclusive Culture," https://www.youtube.com/watch?v=Fi1BLZPtjHA

231. *Profiles in Diversity Journal,* http://www.diversityjournal.com/15214-deborah-gillis-catalyst/

232. ibid

233. Krawcheck, Sallie. 2017. *Own It: The Power of Women at Work.* New York: Crown Business, Kindle, loc 202.

Interactional Leadership

234. Foster, Rebecca. 2016. *Women in Their Own Words: Quotations to Empower and Inspire.* Chichester, England: Summersdale Publishers.

235. El Saadawi, Nawal and Sherif Hatata (translator). 2007. *The Hidden Face of Eve: Women in the Arab World.* Zed Books

236. King, Jeanne Porter. 2014. *Influence to Impact: Leveraging Interpersonal Power for Women's Influence.* Chicago: TransPorter Group Inc.

237. *Grey's Anatomy.* "Something to Talk About." Episode 16. Directed by Adam Davison. Written by Shonda Rhimes and Stacy McKee. ABC, November 6, 2005.

238. Faulkner, Michael Lawrence and Michelle Faulkner-Lunsford. 2014. *Top 100 Power Verbs: The Most Powerful Verbs and Phrases You Can Use to Win in Any Situation.* New Jersey: FT Press.

239. Sharon, Lechte. 2014. *Think and Grow Rich for Women: Using Your Power to Create Success and Significance.* New York: Penguin Random House.

240. Goldsmith, David and Lorrie Goldsmith. 2012. *Paid to Think: A Leader's Toolkit for Redefining Your Future.* Dallas: BenBella Books Inc.

241. Heffernan, Margaret. "Dare to Disagree," TED Talk, June 10, 2015.

242. Fox, Emily Jane. "Mary Barra Opens Up About GM's $500 Million Bet on Lyft." *Vanity Fair,* January 11, 2016, 1:35 p.m., http://www.vanityfair.com/news/2016/01/mary-barra-opens-up-about-gm-bet-on-lyft

243. Singer, June. 1972, 1994. *Boundaries of the Soul: The Practice of Jung's Psychology.* New York: Anchor Books.

244. Schwantes, Marcel. "101 Inspiring Quotes From Trailblazing Women in Honor of Today's Holiday." Inc.com, September 22, 2016

245. Miller, Claire Cain. "Xerox CEO on the Company's 'Earth Shattering Transformation.'" *The New York Times,* October 2, 2012, 8:10 p.m., http://bits.blogs.nytimes.com/2012/10/02/xerox-c-e-o-on-the-companys-earth-shattering-transformation/?_r=0

246. Hesselbein, Frances. 2007. *Hesselbein on Leadership (J-B Leader To Leader Institute).* New York: Jossey-Bass, Kindle Edition, loc 135.

247. Bridges, Frances. "What Madeline Albright Wants Women To Know." *Forbes,* June 24, 2015, http://www.forbes.com/sites/francesbridges/2015/06/24/what-madeline-albright-wants-women-to-know/#3556cc1e64a7

248. Simmons, Annette. 2002, 2006. *Story Factor: Inspiration, Influence, and Persuasion through the Art of Storytelling.* New York: Basic Books.

249. Guiliano, Mireille. "Women, Work and the Art of Savoire Faire Q&A," http://mireilleguiliano.com/content/iwomen-work-art-savoir-fairei-qa

250. Krawcheck, Sallie. 2017. *Own It: The Power of Women at Work.* New York: Crown Business, Kindle, loc 1313.

251. https://www.brainyquote.com/quotes/quotes/s/sarahkay627770.html

252. Sand, George. *Indiana.* 1832, 1994, 2000, 2008. New York: Oxford University.

253. Interview with Marissa Mayer, CEO of Yahoo, EgonZehnder, *The Focus* magazine. http://www.egonzehnder.com/the-focus-magazine/topics/the-focus-on-identity/interview/it-was-a-case-of-getting-focused-on-what-we-could-do-and-then-instilling-a-sense-of-pride.html

254. Simmons, Annette. 2002, 2006. *Story Factor: Inspiration, Influence, and Persuasion through the Art of Storytelling.* New York: Basic Books

255. Commencement address given at Wellesley College, 1996, as quoted in *Way More than*

Luck: Commencement Speeches on Living with Bravery, Empathy, and Other Existential Skills. 2015, Published in 2015 by Chronicle Books LLC, San Francisco.

256. Hendricks, Drew. "15 Quotes from Famous Female CEOs and Entrepreneurs," Inc. com, April 28, 2015, http://www.inc.com/drew-hendricks/15-quotes-from-famous-female-ceos-and-entrepreneurs.html

257. Buchanan, Laurie. 2016. *Note to Self: A Seven-Step Path to Gratitude and Growth.* Berkeley: She Writes Press.

258. Lupton, Rosamund. 2010. *Sister.* New York: Piatkus Books.

259. Jennae, Michele. 2015. *CHARGE! The Patchwork Rhino: A Personal Development Parable.* Michele Jennae Media.

260. Yamanouchi, Miya. 2015. *Embrace Your Sexual Self: A Practical Guide for Women.* Bloomington: Booktango.

261. Mihalic, Mary. 2013. *The 40 Best Business Tips No One's Ever Told You.* Trounce Group LLC.

262. https://www.brainyquote.com/quotes/quotes/c/caitlinmor592711.html

263. Hale, Cynthia. 2010. *I'm a Piece of Work! Sisters Shaped by God.* Valley Forge: Judson Forge, p. 89.

264. Rietzsch, Lindsey K. 2014. *The Happy Lady: Making the Best of What Life Gives Us.* Layton: Visintra Group LLC.

265. Williamson, Marianne. 1993. *A Woman's Worth.* New York: Ballantine Books.

266. Gay, Roxane. "Seeing beyond the workplace," Fortune.com, January 22, 2015, 5:30 a.m.

267. https://www.brainyquote.com/search_results.html?q=margaret+wheatley

268. "Thuli Madonsela: SA's Iron Lady," interview by Corruption Watch, March 8, 2013, 9:27 p.m., http://www.corruptionwatch.org.za/thuli-madonsela-sas-iron-lady/

269. Schanberg, Sydney H. "Indian and Pakistani Armies Confront Each Other Along Borders," *The New York Times*, October 20, 1971, via WikiQuote (as quoted at press conference in New Delhi, October 19, 1971)

270. Venstra, Elizabeth. 2012. *1001 Pearls of Life-Changing Wisdom: Insight on Identity, Truth, and Success.* New York: Skyhorse Publishing.

271. Ravenscraft, Eric. "Don't Be Afraid to Interrupt, If You Know What You're Talking About," Lifehacker.com, June 23, 2015, http://lifehacker.com/dont-be-afraid-to-interrupt-if-you-know-what-youre-tal-1713310409

272. Anderson, Kare. 2014. *Mutuality Matters: How You Can Create More Opportunity, Adventure & Friendship With Others.* Substantium.

273. http://www.goodreads.com/quotes/tag/conversation?page=9

274. Hewlett, Sylvia Ann. 2014. *Executive Presence: The Missing Link Between Merit and Success.* New York: Harper Collins ebooks, p. 24.

Intentional Leadership

275. Yovanoff, Brenna. 2010. *The Replacement.* New York: Razorbill.

276. https://www.brainyquote.com/quotes/quotes/e/eleanorroo164073.html

277. Baxi, Mahesh. 2014. *New Age Leadership.* Mumbai: Jaico Publishing House.

278. Nadela, Timi. 2015. *Get to the Top: It's About the Heart Sell, Not the Hard Sell.* Lioncrest Publishing.

279. "First Lady Says Farewell to the White House: An Oprah Winfrey Special." CBS, (2016)

280. Maxwell, John C. 2003. *Thinking for Change: 11 Ways Highly Successful People Approach Life and Work.* New York: Warner Books.

281. Day, Deborah. 2010, 2015. *Be Happy Now!: Become the Active Director of Your Life*. Xlibris.

282. Karsh, Brad and Courtney Templin. 2013. *Manager 3.0: A Millennial's Guide to Rewriting the Rules of Management*. New York: Amacom.

283. "65 Inspiring Quotes from Strong Women We Love," StyleCaster.com, http://stylecaster.com/beauty/strong-women-quotes/

284. Young Entrepreneur Council. "Best Advice I Ever Got: Catherine Cook." Inc.com, April 20, 2012, http://www.inc.com/young-entrepreneur-council/best-advice-i-ever-got-catherine-cook.html

285. Pearl, Diana. "7 Best Madonna Quotes Ever." Marie Claire.com, July 15, 2014.

286. Niven, Lisa. "On Beauty: Susan Sarandon." *Vogue*, January 8, 2016, http://www.vogue.co.uk/gallery/susan-sarandon-interview-loreal-paris-ambassador

287. Inam, Henna. 2015. *Wired for Authenticity: Seven Practices to Inspire, Adapt & Lead*. Bloomington: iUniverse.

288. Rottenberg, Linda. 2014. *Crazy Is a Compliment: The Power of Zigging When Everyone Else Zags*. New York: Portfolio/Penguin.

289. Hashmi, Hina. 2014. *Your Life: A Practical Guide to Happiness, Peace, and Fulfilment*. UK: For Betterment Publications

290. Hall, Ph.D., Mindy. 2014. *Leading with Intention: Every Moment Is a Choice*. New Hope: Copper Bay Press LLC.

291. Wilson, Donna and Marcus Conyers. 2013. *Five Big Ideas for Effective Teaching: Connecting Mind, Brain, and Education Research to Classroom Practice*. New York: Teachers College Press.

292. Inc.com address given at the Stanford School of Business, quoted in Meg Whitman and the Power of Positivity Inc. May 5, 2016, http://www.inc.com/ilan-mochari/meg-whitman-enduring-legacy-nothing-to-lose.html

293. Pham, Tiffany. "Top 9 Inspirational Quotes by Self-Made Female Moguls," Forbes.com, August 20, 2013, 1:30 a.m., http://www.forbes.com/sites/tiffanypham/2013/08/20/top-9-inspirational-quotes-by-female-moguls/#1ff006544423

294. Twitter, @cristen_rodgers 2:57 p.m., April 25, 2016

295. Zhu, Pearl. 2016. *Digital Valley: Five Pearls of Wisdom to Make Profound Influence*. Book Baby.

296. Tetzlaff, Sue and Jane McLeod. 2016. *The Employee Experience: A Capstone Guide to Peak Performance*. Minneapolis: North Loop Books.

297. Dennis, Trevor A. 2014. *Women Empowerment: A Path to Self-Development and Inspiration for Women*.

298. "65 Inspiring Quotes from Strong Women We Love," StyleCaster.com, http://stylecaster.com/beauty/strong-women-quotes/

299. Rampton, Kristy. "50 Motivational Quotes from Disruptive, trailblazing, Inspiring Women Leaders," May 11, 2015, https://cmoe.com/corporate-strategy/ as quoted in https://www.entrepreneur.com/article/245810

300. Roopleen, Dr. 2013. *Words To inspire the Winner in You*. Power Publishers.

301. Armstrong, Kelley. 2012. *The Calling*. New York: HarperCollins.

302. Salter-McNeil, Brenda. 2015. *Roadmap to Reconciliation: Moving Communities Into Unity, Wholeness and Justice*. Downers Grove: InterVasrity Press, Kindle edition, loc 495.

303. Marti, J.D., Ph.D., Mollie. 2012. *Walking with Justice: Uncommon Lessons from One of Life's Greatest Mentors*. Austin: Greenleaf Book Group Press

304. Harris, Carla A. 2009. *Expect to Win: Proven Strategies for Success from a Wall Street Vet*. New York: Hudson Street Press.

305. https://www.goodreads.com/author/show/6593289.K_L_Toth

306. Yovanoff, Brenna. 2010. *The Replacement*. New York: Razorbill.

307. Hall, Ph.D., Mindy. 2014. *Leading with Intention: Every Moment Is a Choice*. Copper Bay Press LLC

308. Rampton, Kristy. "50 Motivational Quotes from Disruptive, Trailblazing, Inspiring Women Leaders," May 11, 2015, https://www.entrepreneur.com/article/245810

309. http://www.ameliaearhart.com/about/quotes.html

310. Maxwell, John C. 2005. *The Choice Is Yours: Today's Decisions for the Rest of Your Life*. Nashville: Thomas Nelson Book Group.

311. Emling, Shelley. 2012. *Marie Curie and Her Daughters: The Private Lives of Science's First Family*. New York: St. Martin's Press.

312. McKenzie, Vashti M. 1996. *Not Without a Struggle, Leadership Development for African American Women in Ministry*. Cleveland: Pilgrim Press.

313. Johnson, Whitney L. 2015. *Disrupt Yourself: Putting the Power of Disruptive Innovation to Work*. Routledge

314. Naslund, Sena Jeter. 1999, 2005. *Ahab's Wife: or, The Star-Gazer*. New York: HarperCollins.

315. Pham, Tiffany. "Top 9 Inspirational Quotes by Self-Made Female Moguls," Forbes. com, August 20, 2013, 1:30 a.m., http://www.forbes.com/sites/tiffanypham/2013/08/20/top-9-inspirational-quotes-by-female-moguls/#1ff006544423

316. Black, Lee Bob. "50+ Inspiring Quotes by Women: Women's History Month," March 11, 2015, Skilledup.com, http://www.skilledup.com/articles/inspiring-quotes-womens-history-month

317. https://hbr.org/2015/09/how-indra-nooyi-turned-design-thinking-into-strategy

318. Hay House. "Oh The Thinks you can Think!." Heal Your Life Blog, March 1, 2013, 3:45 a.m., http://www.healyourlife.com/oh-the-thinks-you-can-think

319. McKenzie, Vashti M. 1996, 2011. *Not Without a Struggle, Leadership Development for African American Women in Ministry*. Cleveland: Pilgrim Press, Kindle edition, loc 107.

320. Cottrill, Mike. "Donna E. Shalala." *Smart Business*, April 26, 2007, http://www.sbnonline.com/article/donna-e-shalala-president-university-of-miami/

321. McKenzie, Vashti M. 1996, 2011. *Not Without a Struggle, Leadership Development for African American Women in Ministry*. Cleveland: Pilgrim Press, Kindle edition, loc 2612.

Connective Leadership

322. Caproni, Ph.D., Paula J. 2017. *The Science of Success: What Researchers Know that You Should Know*. U.S.: Van Rye Publishing, LLC

323. Barrett, Morag. 2014. *Cutlivate: The Power of Winning Relationships*. Austin: Greenleaf Book Group Press.

324. Weems, Renita. 2002. *Showing Mary: How Women Can Share Prayers, Wisdom and the Blessings of God*. New York: Walk Worthy Press, Kindle edition, loc 319.

325. Follett, Mary Parker. 1971. *Creative Experience*. New York: Peter Smith, p. 301.

326. IIT commencement address given May 16, 2009 by Marissa Mayer in Chicago, Illinois.

327. Rich, Adrienne. 1983. *Sources*. Heyeck Press

328. Rowe, Nikki. 2013. *Once a Girl, Now a Woman*. Bloomington: Balboa Press

329. Day M.A, Deborah. 2015. *Be Happy Now! Become the Active Director of Your Life*. Xlibris

330. Katehakis, Alexandra and Tom Bliss. 2014. *Mirror of Intimacy: Daily Reflections on Emotional and Erotic Intelligence*. Los Angeles: Center for Healthy Sex.

331. Sotomayor, Sonia. 2013. *My Beloved World.* New York: Knopf.

332. Hampton, Kathy (aka Kathy Bee). 2014. *Footsteps My Journey: The True Story About the Beloved Poem Footprints in the Sand.* Amazon Kindle.

333. Sayers, Dorothy L. 1936, 1964, 1987, 1993, 2012. *Gaudy Night.* New York: HarperCollins.

334. White, Kate. 2012. *I Shouldn't Be Telling You This: Success Secrets Every Gutsy Girl Should Know.* New York: HarperCollins.

335. Wein, Elizabeth. 2013. *Rose Under Fire,* New York: Hyperion.

336. Morris, Alex. "Ballerina Misty Copeland on Breaking Barriers and Loving Her Strong Body," Glamour.com, October 29, 2015, 3:45 p.m., http://www.glamour.com/story/misty-copeland

337. Kidd, Sue Monk. 2002. *The Secret Life of Bees.* New York: Penguin Books.

338. St. John, Bonnie and Darcy Deane. 2012. *How Great Women Lead: A Mother-Daughter Adventure into the Lives of Women Shaping the World.* New York: Center Street (Hachette Book Group).

339. Walker, Chariss K. 2016. *Keep the Faith.* Books Mango (Createspace Direct).

340. Goodrich, Richelle E. 2015. *Making Wishes: Quotes, Thoughts & a Little Poetry for Every Day of the Year.* Createspace.

341. Guiliano, Miereille. 2009. *Women, Work & the Art of Savoir-Faire: Business Sense and Sensibility.* New York: Atria Books

342. Lily Tomlin and Jane Fonda, "A Hilarious Celebration of Lifelong Friendship." TED Talk, December 2015.

343. ibid.

344. Handler, Chelsea. "We Have a Problem with Women Supporting Women," December 11, 2014, https://journal.thriveglobal.com/chelsea-handler-we-have-a-problem-with-women-supporting-women-a60e6de13d15#.95n6gh5v5, Thriveglobal.com

345. Lily Tomlin and Jane Fonda, "A Hilarious Celebration of Lifelong Friendship." TED Talk, December 2015.

346. Amy Poehler, "You Can't Do It Alone," Class Day at Harvard University, May 25, 2015, http://harvardmagazine.com/2011/05/you-cant-do-it-alone

347. Kingsolver, Barbara. 1998, 2002. *The Poisonwood Bible.* New York: HarperPerennial.

348. "55 Inspiring Friendship Quotes." YourTango.com, http://www.yourtango.com/2013190143/37-friendship-quotes-famous-inspirational-best-friends-sayings

349. "Mary Barra, GM's New Chief, Speaking Her Mind," *The New York Times,* December 10, 2013, http://www.nytimes.com/2013/12/11/business/mary-barra-gms-new-chief-speaking-her-mind.html

350. Shambora, Jessica. "Xerox's Next CEO: Ursula Burns," Fortune.com, May 22, 2009, 5:24 p.m. MDT, http://fortune.com/2009/05/22/xeroxs-next-ceo-ursula-burns/

351. Jensen, Cordelia. 2015. *Skyscraping.* New York: Philomel Books.

352. Kaye, Beverly, and Julie Winkle Giulioni. 2012. *Help them Grow or Watch them Go: Career Conversations Employees Want.* San Francisco: Berrett-Koehler Publishers.

353. Remarks by First Lady Michelle Obama at the National Mentoring Summit, January 25, 2011, Library of Congress, Washington, D.C.

354. Pittman, Taylor. "Laura and Barbara Bush Open Up About Family, Gender Roles, and Learning About 9/11." *The Huffington Post,* April 25, 2016. http://www.huffingtonpost.com/entry/laura-bush-shares-with-her-daughter-the-moment-she-learned-about-911_us_570eae60e4b08a2d32b8e6e3

355. Rosenbaum, Judith. "Adrienne Rich: navigating hope," JWA.org, March 29, 2012,

https://jwa.org/blog/adrienne-rich-navigating-hope

356. Harris, Carla A. 2009. *Expect to Win: 10 Proven Strategies for Thriving in the Workplace*. New York: Hudson Street Press, p. 171.

357. Cleveland, Cristena. 2013. *Disunity in Christ: Uncovering the Hidden Forces that Keep Us Apart*. Downers Grove: IVP Books, p. 42.

358. Hyun, Jane. 2005. *Breaking the Bamboo Ceiling: Career Strategies for Asians*. New York: HarperCollins.

359. Goodrich, Richelle E. 2015. *Making Wishes: Quotes, Thoughts & a Little Poetry for Every Day of the Year*. Createspace.

360. DeMuth, Mary E. 2012. *Everything: What You Give and What You Gain to Become Like Jesus*. Nashville: Thomas Nelson.

361. Berrien, Elizabeth. 2013. *Creative Grieving: A Hip Chick's Path from Loss to Hope*. Austin: River Grove Books.

362. Lindsey, Connie. "Life Lessons from the C-Suite," http://www.socialifechicago.com/2016/10/24/life-lessons-from-the-c-suite-connie-lindsey/

363. Harris, Carla A. 2009. *Expect to Win: 10 Proven Strategies for Thriving in the Workplace*. New York: Hudson Street Press, p. 115.

364. Debbye Turner Bell on running a marathon with a friend, http://debbyeturner.com/marathon.html

365. Hale, Mandy. 2013. *The Single Woman: Life, Love, and a Dash of Sass*. Nashville: Thomas Nelson.

366. McKenzie, Vashti. M. 1996, 2011. *Not Without a Struggle: Leadership Development for African American Women In Ministry*. Cleveland: Pilgrim Press, Kindle edition, loc 2664.